HOW TO WRITE AN ASTROLOGICAL SYNTHESIS

A guide for students

by

TERRY DWYER, M.A., D.M.S. Astrol.

L.N.Fowler & Co Ltd
1201/3 High Road
Chadwell Heath
Romford Essex RM6 4DH

CONTENTS

INTRODUCTION

As the subtitle indicates, this is a book intended primarily for students of astrology, and it is conceived and worded accordingly: however, I believe that many experienced astrologers might benefit from reading it and adopting some of its methods. I feel that there is a real need for a book like this because so much astrological literature has been devoted to unravelling the individual meanings of the things found in a birthchart, but little or nothing to the verbal end product, as seen by the client or conveyed to him face-to-face. In fact the whole astrological world seems careless of the need to synthesise: lip-service is paid to it, but interpretations so often refer to individual sections of the chart, disregarding other chart factors which may in fact compensate. Phrases like "Your Scorpio Ascendant makes you intense" or "You're shy, aren't you? I expect you've got Moon conjunct Saturn" are to be heard even (especially?) at astrology conferences. Most astrologers seem positively unable to refer to a human trait without promptly sticking a simple astrological label on it, yet traits are not normally to be associated with a single chart factor. *Only the whole chart should be considered, for any astrological purpose whatever*. Of course there will always be controversy about what constitutes "the whole chart"....

And I must also add a very important rider: a really complete synthesis requires not only the birthchart but as much background knowledge of the native and his circumstances as possible. Nature, nurture, willpower and choice all play their part. However, students (and sometimes practising astrologers) are often required to interpret a chart without being supplied with any further information. (Certainly I have had more than my fair share of clients who never meet me, nor tell

1

me anything about themselves.) Such "blind" astrology is not an ideal way of helping the client but it is an ideal way of testing how far you have learnt your craft. For that reason I believe that all astrologers should attempt it from time to time. But blind chart interpretation is unlikely to be successful if it is not done methodically and carefully.

So proper synthesis should apply to all forms of astrology, for example synastry, and the interpretation of progressions and transits. The latter particularly should involve a synthesis of the transits, not only with each other but with everything in the natal chart. Current books don't show how to do this, nor even stress its need. Maybe such a book will get written soon; in the meanwhile I can hope that the methods expounded in these pages might provide enough hints for the better execution of such tasks.

Finally, I would like to thank Tony Martin and Lindsey Holleworth for reading the script of this book and for making valuable suggestions.

T.D. January, 1985.

CHAPTER 1

UNDERSTANDING THE TASK

WHERE HELP IS NEEDED

All students of astrology need help with synthesis. There are dozens of books available on chart interpretation, but these normally deal with analysis, not synthesis. I have never come across a single book devoted to this latter subject, in spite of some mistitled books which appear to be. The best we have seems to be a chapter "Scheme of Chart Interpretation, with Example" in Margaret Hone's "Modern Textbook of Astrology". I have to acknowledge my indebtedness to this author and particularly to this chapter which I, as a student, found extremely enlightening and which first put me on the right road where synthesis was concerned. (And there are further examples in Hone's "Applied Astrology".) However, for all its virtues, Hone's exposition is incomplete and still leaves much to the student's initiative. It is a signpost rather than a route map, and so in this book I hope to provide rather more information for the lost traveller.

My experiences in talking to astrology students, and more importantly, teaching them, leave me in no doubt that synthesis is the one thing that they find the hardest, indeed I have seen more students give up astrology, or at least astrology courses, because of its difficulties, than for any other reason. Even Diploma-holders have confided to me that they still find it a problem, or even a nightmare! Yet anyone with reasonable intelligence, some command of English, and willingness to practise, can learn to write a good synthesis. They don't even need to know any astrology!

4

TERMINOLOGY

I had better explain that last astonishing-sounding claim, above. There has always been a lack of agreement among astrologers about what to call the end product of the full interpretation of a natal chart. It has been called variously an interpretation, a reading, a chart analysis, an astro-analysis, a synthesis or chart synthesis, not to mention such ill-defined phrases as "doing a chart". And of course the word horoscope is often used for this purpose, though it really refers to the chart itself.

The first confusion to clear up is the use of the words analysis and synthesis, which are clear opposites, analysis meaning a taking apart, synthesis a blending together, like assembling jigsaw pieces correctly to form a meaningful picture. It is not correct to speak of a full interpretation as an analysis: this suggests an incomplete job, where the native is presented with the jigsaw set and invited to make his own picture. Nevertheless we do use analysis as part of our work: but we analyse the chart (horoscope) into its components; it is the meanings we synthesise. And of course there has to be an intermediate process which translates the chart factors into meanings. Somewhat thus:

Chart – ANALYSIS – Factors (Signs, aspects, etc) – INTERPRETATION – Meanings – SYNTHESIS – Final result

In the above "process stream" the three vital processes are in capitals. So there can be no synthesis until there has been analysis. If we had left out interpretation, that would have meant putting the chart factors back into order *as* chart factors, much as if we had reshuffled the planets and houses etc. around to produce a new chart. Pointless! (Except in such things as harmonics, which virtually does something rather like that.) The real crux, of course, is the interpretation process, which changes astrological concepts such as Moon in Capricorn to psychological concepts such as pennypinching, now written down as notes, phrases, sentences, etc. These latter are what need synthesis, and this final process is what causes so much trouble to students of astrology. The rewards are great, however: it was a chart that was analysed, but it is a person that is being synthesised (or rather, a portrait of a person.)

So, as we look at the process stream again:

1) Chart
2) ANALYSIS
3) Factors
4) INTERPRETATION
5) Meanings
6) SYNTHESIS
7) Final result

we see that (provided an astrologer did the work as far as 5) anyone expert in the process of synthesis could complete the job, even with no knowledge of astrology. But obviously astrologers don't wish to farm out the third process to someone else!

There remains the problem of what to call the final result. The word synthesis, according to the dictionary, may correctly be used to describe either the process or its own product, but this might confuse the learner. Also, the names using the word "analysis" are inappropriate. "Full interpretation" is fairly innocuous though a trifle clumsy-sounding. I cannot pretend to have found the ideal name; but for the purposes of this book I shall use the term Final Report, so that the word synthesis can be reserved to mean the process of putting meanings together: however, in the world at large, I see no great harm in using Synthesis (or Horoscope) to mean this end product.

I am also working on the assumption that this Final Report will be in written form. Even if you wish to give it orally, the principles of arriving at it are the same; and in any case it is advisable for learners to practise actually writing their reports until they are expert. There is something beautifully uncompromising about a written report: there it all is in black and white; you are committed to definite statements which you cannot wriggle out of! And it is easier to forge a written report into a pleasingly organised, literate and logical form than it is when speaking. I hasten to add that I am fully aware of the value of face-to-face astrological counselling. But it can only be an advantage to start the latter from the basis of a properly written Final Report, even if this is modified when delivered orally to the client. Giving an oral interpretation direct from the chart is full of pitfalls, and you should refuse to do it if pressured - at least if the interpretation is meant as definitive: there is little harm in interpreting direct from the chart as a student exercise, provided it is realised that this is analysis, not synthesis.

PRACTICAL DIFFICULTIES
This book will offer help at all stages of the interpretation process, not only at the synthesis stage, though I will be concentrating on that. It seems to me that the difficulties normally encountered can be listed as follows:

1) Knowing which chart factors to use
2) Attaching the right degree of importance to each factor
3) Finding the right interpretations for each factor
4) Reconciling contradictions
5) Placing the right degree of emphasis or weighting on different traits
6) Wording the synthesised notes into coherent, stylish and useful sentences
7) Arranging the latter in a logical and meaningful sequence

These are the main difficulties, though there are plenty of minor ones, too. The remaining chapters of this book will attempt to solve the problems raised by these difficulties. Those who feel they are already expert in analysis and interpretation may skip to Chapter 4 for advice on synthesis proper.

CHAPTER 2

ANALYSIS (1): CHART FACTORS

WHAT IS THE CHOICE?
Geoffrey Dean, in "Recent Advances in Natal Astrology", has highlighted the problem of the "super-chart" which contains so many factors ("significators") that the astrologer is faced with chaos; and we are all in danger of following the motto "If it moves, interpret it": or worse, "If it can be put in the chart, interpret it".

Yet it is to some extent understandable that beginners should be tempted to include as many things in the scheme as possible. For one thing they will have read about them, and so feel guilty if they omit them; for another, they are often at a loss to get sufficient meaning from a relatively small number of things, so they imagine that by including more and more factors they will get closer and closer to the truth. Alas, they are more likely to get further from it. I speak feelingly, as one who has wasted as much time on non-essentials as anybody. Nowadays I use only signs and aspects, nothing else, having discarded houses (with a great sense of relief) two or three years ago, and other odds and ends long before that. (I have a strange feeling that I might discard signs one day, too.)

I do not expect that many people will go as far as I have in this direction, but I do say this: if you have any sneaking feeling that you are including certain things in order to fill up gaps, try a different approach: instead of using more and more things to mean less and less, use fewer and fewer things to mean more and more. By which I mean that we should learn to "squeeze the juice" from the few really useful things. So use whatever you feel is right and proper to use, but be sure you

7

are exploiting it to the full, and be sure that you are putting the right weight on it, too.

DON'T DUPLICATE

My main objection to counting the elements, for example, is that we shall in any case be interpreting the planets by sign, so any preponderance or lack is automatically taken care of. For example, once you have interpreted Ascendant, Sun, Mercury, Venus, and Mars (not to mention Uranus and Pluto) all in Leo, as in one chart in my collection, the emphasis on Fire and Fixity has been dealt with. The portrait of this person must be looking decidedly Leonian before we get any further! If we now also say "This chart has 6 planets and the Ascendant in Fire Signs" there is no harm if we merely SAY it, but to interpret it, and to add this interpretation to what we have already, is to make the elementary error of doing the job twice. Thus we overemphasise. There is a more subtle danger in dealing with missing elements: the same chart has nothing in Water, as it happens. Again, no harm in noticing this, but to write down "Lacks feeling, imagination etc" is to overemphasies what already exists, namely a dearth of statements involving these qualities. Leave it to take care of itself.

ASPECT PATTERNS

Another common form of duplication is to interpret such patterns as T-squares, etc. There's really no need! You will be in any case (one hopes) interpreting the three aspects comprising the T-square, each separately: thus the sum total of the pattern's meaning will have been arrived at by interpreting the three aspects. If you now go on to interpret the T-squares as if it were something additional, again there is duplication, and overemphasis in the Final Report. Obviously the same applies to any pattern: Grand Cross, Grand Trine, Satellitium, etc.

SIGNS IN ASPECT

A more subtle form of duplication comes from over-assiduousness in interpreting aspects, by constantly taking the sign into consideration. Suppose we have Mars squaring the Sun, sextiling Jupiter, and opposite Moon. Mars is in Sagittarius, let us say. One way to interpret the aspects is to say "First we have Mars in Sagittarius squaring Sun in Pisces: this particular square will therefore be Mutable in colour, and actions will be evasive, intermittent, trial-and-error in nature, and suchlike. Then we have Mars in Sagittarius sextile Jupiter in Libra, so actions will be scattered and far-reaching, varied social life is likely, lots of travel, etc. Finally the Moon in Gemini opposite the Sagittarian Mars gives an emotional kick to the actions which will tend to be diffuse in purpose, though enthusiastic." This is all based on sound astrological principles, but in fact it is well on the way to interpreting Mars in Sagittarius three times over (or even four times including the presumed separate interpretation of Mars in Sagittarius). This of course is unfair to those planets with fewer aspects!

Duplication is rife, and the Final Report will be unbalanced accordingly. (There is no harm in this kind of thing if one is interpreting an aspect on its own, out of context, but if we are considering the interpretation of a complete chart, it is wrong.)

CHART SHAPES
I will consider only two of these for the purposes of illustration, but the principle applies to them all.

The Bundle Shape, where all the planets are contained within an angle of about 120 degrees, is supposed to make the native narrow or one-sided, or let us say concentrated in outlook. But since the signs (and houses) occupied by the planets are in any case few in number, we will have covered that by the straightforward interpretation of the individual planets by sign, or by house. Don't do it a second time!

Likewise a man with a Splash shaped chart will have a high number of sign (or house) interpretations to his credit, making him versatile, or wide in his interests. No need to say, over and above this: "The Splash shape gives him wide interests".

SUMMARY
What all these warnings about duplication add up to is this: interpret the signs (and houses, if you wish), also the aspects; and the rest will take care of itself. Element preponderance/-lack, aspect patterns, shapes, etc will *automatically* be covered.

Are you a duplicator? Can you think of other ways in which you may have been guilty of duplication? Can you think of any ways in which the chart forms you use encourage you to duplicate? Once you can overcome a guilty conscience about leaving many of the spaces on a chart form blank, you will never look back!

To be more specific, I recommend that you interpret the following in a chart:

1) Ascendant by sign.
2) Planets Sun to Saturn by sign.
3) Planets Sun to Pluto by house, if you wish to use houses.
4) All aspects between planets.
5) A careful consideration of unaspected or very weakly aspected planets.

I omit interpretation of MC by sign because I am not convinced that it has any effect: by all means include it if you know what you are doing. I also omit interpretations of Uranus, Neptune and Pluto by sign because of the "generation" effect, but they can be included so long as they are played down sufficiently. Nor do I use aspects to Angles, as I am not only unconvinced of their effectiveness (other than conjunctions, which give angularity) but am not satisfied that really useful meanings can be found for them. Again, go ahead if you feel happy with them. (But please say "conjunct Descendant" rather than "opposite Ascendant" and you will be more likely to interpret correctly: similarly with the MC/IC.)

Advice on interpreting unaspected planets will be found on page 25.

CHAPTER 3

ANALYSIS (2): FINDING INTERPRETATIONS

Having decided on which chart factors we are going to use, our next problem is to interpret them. Before going any further I would like to make one thing very clear: at this stage we shall be interpreting each factor *in isolation*, without regard to whatever else is in the chart. This may surprise some readers, who are accustomed to reading such phrases as "Much will depend on the rest of the map"; "Unless the horoscope contains other mitigating features..."; "A strong Saturn in the horoscope negates this danger"; "...can be drastically ruined unless the chart has redeeming features." But the danger we have to guard against is premature synthesis. Synthesis *will* be done when the time comes; but if we start making all sorts of allowances already, we shall all too easily lose track of ourselves and do the job again later - another case of duplication! So bear in mind that the interpretation of each chart factor should be undertaken (to begin with) as if it were the *only* feature of the chart. Don't worry if it contradicts something else you can see out of the corner of your eye: stick to one thing at a time.

So we can afford to take interpretations at their face value, for now. But from what source do we derive our meanings? I can think of several:

1) "Cookbooks" (Textbooks with meanings tabulated under headings)
2) Textbooks in general (various meanings, untabulated, which one picks up and somehow learns)
3) Personal teachers (likely to be similar to 2) in nature)

4) Personal experience, from many charts (unlikely at first, of course)
5) Keywords and commonsense
6) Intuition

Possibly you are using all of the above methods to some degree or other, and indeed it is difficult not to, after a while. There is something to be said for each method, but there are concomitant dangers, too: mainly that of too great a dependence on someone else, or something unreliable. "Cookbooks" can be good, *if* you know you have a thoroughly reliable one (I have not found one yet). Intuition *may* save the day, but it is often guesswork, or even laziness, masquerading as knowledge. I am going to suggest 5) above, as the best starting-point for a full and intelligent method. To quote Margaret Hone: "To begin with, such notes must be made by looking up... (cookbook meanings)." This is tedious. The only way to avoid it is by *work*. So let us see how we can interpret from keywords.

INTERPRETATION FROM KEYWORDS
Without a knowledge of keyword meanings for planets, signs, houses, aspects, etc. you are unlikely to get far. This approach to learning astrology, pioneered by Margaret Hone and since followed by many astrology teachers, has the advantage of simplicity and relative ease of learning. It has the difficulty that each individual must find his own way of expanding these keywords into concepts, phrases, etc. This may be a difficulty but it is not a drawback, for each budding astrologer must learn to fashion his own talents in the way that he can best use them, not slavishly to ape someone else whose methods suit only his own personality, or who may even be in error. So learn your keywords!

The process of expanding keywords can be likened to a pyramid. On top sits *the* keyword - that one word (if it can be found) which best summarises and encapsulates the essence of the symbol. (E.g. Saturn = Restriction). Below the top stone come a small group of "subheadings" which are one remove from, or primary divisions of, the main keyword. Thus for Saturn we might have Delay, Self-control, Illness, Setback. Then below these again we can have further subdivisions such as Old Men, Maturity, Incarceration, Chronic diseases, and so on. (See Appendix for lists of keywords.) At any one time in your development as an astrologer you will know a given number of keywords for each factor, perhaps only one at first: but as your experience grows, so that number will grow too. The more keywords you have learnt, the better your interpretation and Final Report will be. But this pyramidal effect exists, not only in the structure of the learnt keywords, but in the manner of expanding those which are known: again using the Saturn example, you should think of all the forms of restriction that could possibly apply to a human being: not only illness or imprisonment but lack of opportunity, stifled ambitions, psychological inhibitions, interference from others, excessive caution, and so on. But as we shall very soon see, such inventive expansion will operate more easily when we are combining two astrological symbols.

THE "KEYWORD GRID"
Of course one is never interpreting a single astrological factor such as Saturn: it is always Saturn in Libra or Saturn opposite Uranus, and so on. So we normally deal with *two* concepts in combination. It would be possible to combine three things together, but (except in the case of midpoint combinations) this is too confusing and I do not advise it. So if Saturn is in Libra in the 11th house, opposite Uranus, we should interpret Saturn in Libra, Saturn in 11th house, and Saturn opposite Uranus, all separately, at first. Remember, we are at the analysis stage, not the synthesis, yet. (Though I have to admit that just to say Saturn in Libra is already a kind of synthesis.)

The way to come up with the meanings of a 2-factor combination (note that I say meanings, not meaning) is as follows:

1) Write down all the keywords you know for the first factor
   (say 4 for example)
2) Write down all the keywords you know for the other factor
   (say 5)
3) Make out a grid on paper, consisting of large squares, 4 x
   5, with margins.
4) Write your first lot of keywords across the top, and your
   second lot down the lefthand side, in the margins.
5) Fill in each square by combining the two marginal
   keywords together.

An example should make this clear. Suppose we are interpreting Moon in Taurus, and we know the following keywords for Moon: Habits, Emotions, Routine, Mother; also
the following for Taurus: Stable, Reliable, Patient, Slow,
Boring. Then our grid will look like this:

	1. Habits	2.Emotions	3. Routine	4.Mother
1 Stable	Stable habits	Stable emotions	Stable routine	Stable mother
2 Reliable	Rel. habits	Rel. emotions	Rel. routine	Rel. mother
3 Patient	Patient habits	Patient emots.	Pat. routine	Patient mother
4 Slow	Slow habits	Slow emotions	Slow routine	Slow mother
5 Boring	Boring habits	Boring emotions	Boring routine	Boring mother

We now need to look closely at all these phrases to see what
we can make of them. They are extremely stilted, and in some
cases cryptic, at the moment, so we shall translate them,
where possible, into something of more immediate useful-
ness. I will run through all 20 of these, to see what I can make
of them. Please follow this process closely.

1/1 Stable habits = Will not change habits easily: may even be
a "creature of habit" unable to adapt to unusual situations.

1/2 Stable emotions = not moved easily, but when moved,
may carry the feeling for a long while.

1/3 Stable routine = Will prefer to follow a well-established
pattern of daily life, work, etc. (Similar to 1/1).

1/4 Stable mother = Regards his mother as stable, and his
relationship with her as one not easily upset.

2/1 Reliable habits = Is normally reliable; can be relied on to exhibit his usual habits.

2/2 Reliable emotions (Not really meaningful. It will not do to interpret this as "Having predictable emotions" because "reliable", in the Taurean sense, is not equivalent to "predictable".)

2/3 Reliable routine = Can be depended on when carrying out routine tasks.

2/4 Reliable mother = Sees his mother as a reliable person.

3/1 Patient habits = Is normally patient

3/2 Patient emotions (Meaningless)

3/3 Patient routine = Carries out routine jobs in a patient manner

3/4 Patient mother = Sees his mother as patient.

4/1 Slow habits = Is habitually slow in action.

4/2 Slow emotions = Slow to react emotionally, e.g. diffficult to rouse to anger.

4/3 Slow routine = Prefers jobs in which he can take his time.

4/4 Slow mother (Pass.)

5/1 Boring habits = Too entrenched in habits: may irritate others because of this.

5/2 Boring emotions (Pass)

5/3 Boring routine = Suitable for repetitive or menial jobs.

5/4 Boring mother = Sees his mother as boring.

Several points emerge from the exercise. One is the obvious one that certain combinations do not seem to produce anything meaningful. This is fairly normal, and to some extent depends on what basic keywords were chosen in the first place.

Some pairs of meanings seem fairly close to each other, eg. those involving habits and routine. This is because habits and routine are similar in meaning anyway. We could have saved time, perhaps, by using habits/routine as one keyword from the beginning. Nevertheless it often happens in practice that the same meaning is thrown up in two or more places in the grid: this must be reduced to one, or we shall be duplicating.

Another point concerns the mother. It is often stated that the Moon in a chart describes the mother, but this is not true, for the chart applies only to the native, the mother being described by her own chart. So in the above example the native's mother may not actually be stable, etc. at all—this depends on her own chart—but we can infer that he projects Taurean qualities upon her—he sees her as a Taurean; modified of course by whatever aspects the Moon receives.

But, even allowing for the above snags, we have a very useful method of evolving multiple meanings from a few keywords. At least 15 meanings stand up to scrutiny from the original 20 (4 x 5). So, if you know say 10 keywords for a planet and 10 for a sign, house or another planet, you immediately command 100 meanings in theory, of which maybe 75 should make sense. At this rate, with Ascendant and 7 planets in signs, 10 planets in houses, and say 16 aspects in a chart, you have 2550 likely meanings at your fingertips, and all without bringing in chart shapes, element counts, asteroids, nodes, retrogrades and the rest! Do you now understand my earlier advice on keeping chart factors to a proved minimum, on the grounds that we will be able to get plenty of meanings from them? More and more from less and less!

Of course the number of keywords will not always be 10; the number of duds will vary, and so on: but the method is there, and proves that with adequate keyword meanings, we have no need of cookbooks: in fact we could write our own. If you feel that you cannot produce about 10 keywords for every-thing, then go on learning until you can. Even whilst your output may be small, you can still use the grid method; and as your repertoire expands, so will your powers of interpretation.

Having drawn my squares in a grid for the sake of illustration, I can now say that in practice we need not bother to do this (the paper is never big enough anyway) but we can simply list them, to form what I call a keyword ladder. Start with the two lists of keywords and work your way through the combinations, amplifying as you go. Where no meaning appears to make sense, simply omit. So the best way of working our previous example is actually this:

Moon in Taurus
Moon keywords: Habits, Emotions, Routine, Mother.
Taurus keywords: Stable, Reliable, Patient, Slow, Boring

1) Stable habits = Will not change habits easily: may be creature of habit.
2) Stable emotions = Not moved easily
                     Keeps emotions when roused.
3) Stable routine = 1)
4) Stable mother = Regards mother as dependable.

And so on.

Notice how in 2) the two meanings are put on separate lines. This is because we may want to split these remarks later, so we need to see them as individual entities.

You may like to try an exercise or two before reading further, to be sure that the "grid" method is grasped. Try one or two planets in signs or houses, and one or two aspects. (Don't worry about the nature of the aspect yet.) Draw the grid if you think it helps, or use the listing method above. As you get more proficient, omit keywords entirely, and simply list meanings under the planet headings.

WHICH MEANINGS APPLY?
One of the most frequent queries I get from students, either early on, or when this listing stage is reached, is "But how do I know which of all these possible meanings applies to the native in question?" (And of course this same query arises if cookbooks are used). The answer is a simple one: *all* of them. We cannot afford to rule out anything yet. Remember this is analysis, not synthesis. When we get to the latter, we shall sort out the wheat from the chaff, but at present we have no way of knowing which is which. So down they all go! And don't worry if there are only a few, because of your restricted knowledge of keywords. The correct principle is being used, and experience will increase your powers.

WHAT ABOUT DUPLICATED MEANINGS?
Sooner or later the same meaning will crop up a second or third time. What do we do? Well, my immediate reaction is, for heaven's sake don't cross one out! (Unless it occurs within the same grid, as sometimes happens.) If a meaning occurs more than once, *from different chart sources*, then that is of importance: again, things will get sorted out later. This kind of repetitive emphasis will obviously help us with the selecting process.

INTERPRETING ASPECTS
The procedure for aspects in very similar, but with one important difference. With a planet in a sign, I regard the sign as an adjective modifying the noun provided by the planet. (Strictly it should be an adverb modifying a verb.) But two planets in aspect each modify the other, so we really ought to treat the keyword combinations twice over, if we are to exhaust the possibilities. Follow this example:

Venus aspecting Saturn
Venus words: Beauty, Love, Cooperation, Pleasure.
Saturn words: Discipline, Duty, Conventionality, Delay.

1) Beautiful discipline (meaningless)
   Disciplined beauty = Prefers austere art, would plan pictures carefully (if artistic), etc. Tidy with clothes.
2) Beautiful Duty (meaningless)
   Dutiful Beauty (meaningless)
3) Beautiful Conventionality (meaningless)
   Conventional beauty = Has orthodox tastes in furniture, decor, clothes, etc.
4) Beautiful delay (meaningless)
   Delayed beauty = The ugly duckling who achieves grace after a bad start.
5) Loving Discipline = Would be strict but merciful towards his children Ditto with employees
   Disciplined Love = Would not give love to all and sundry. Could not express love in a free, uninhibited fashion.
6) Loving duty = Performs duties willingly and as a gift to loved ones.
   Dutiful love = Giving love seen as a duty. Can be relied on to remember birthdays and anniversaries.
7) Loving conventionality (meaningless)
   Conventional love = Few affairs.
                       Loyal to one partner.
                       Normal marriage pattern.
                       Sexually unadventurous.
8) Loving delay (meaningless)
   Delayed love = Slow to fall in love.
                  Marriage comparatively late in life, maybe after a difficult search for a partner.
9) Cooperative discipline = Able to accept necessary rules and regulations.
                            Probably democratic by inclination.

Disciplined cooperation = Similar to above.
10) Cooperative duty = Will do duty in order to maintain peace.
    Dutiful cooperation = Similar.
11) Cooperative conventionality = Toes the line when in company: tends to go along with the herd.
    Conventional cooperation = Similar.
12) Cooperative delay (meaningless)
    Delayed cooperation = Will want to fall in line with others but may take his time about joining in. ("I will if the others will")
13) Pleasant discipline (meaningless)
    Disciplined pleasure = Liking for sports with well-defined rules.
    Membership of well-structured societies.
14) Pleasant duty = Tries to enjoy carrying out duties.
    Dutiful pleasure = May go to parties and other entertainments because he feels it is good for him.
15) Pleasant conventionality = Predictable but nice with it, i.e. not boringly predictable: does all the "right things".
    Conventional pleasure = No hang-gliding, mountaineering, archaeology; more likely pub visits, cinema, television, outings to stately homes.
16) Pleasant delay (meaningless)
    Delayed pleasure = Probably works hard in youth to build a good future, promising himself a good time when he has earned it.
    Savours his food rather than gulping it.

Of course other keywords can be used to amplify the interpretation of this aspect. Do you notice that most of the useful meanings came from the second of each pair? Although to get the fullest possible interpretation we need to consider the keyword-pairs both ways round; in practice the majority will be easily derived by putting the outer planet first, as an adjective, and the inner planet second, as a noun. If you are in a hurry, use this method and there will be little you will miss. In fact, I find the following table very useful for getting things started:

	Adjective	**Noun**
Sun	(Conscious)	Nature
Moon	Instinctive	Habits
Mercury	Thoughtful	Thinking
Venus	Harmonious	Love
Mars	Active	Action
Jupiter	Expansive	Expansion
Saturn	Controlled	Control
Uranus	Unconventional	Reform
Neptune	Idealised	Idealism
Pluto	Drastic	(Intensification)

Examples: Venus/Saturn = Controlled love.   Mars/Pluto = Drastic action; Sun/Mercury = Thoughtful nature.

Once again, note that the best way is to put the second planet first, for this purpose.

FURTHER REFINEMENT
Although about 75 meanings per factor has been mentioned as a figure, this is more theoretical than practical, so we can set our sights lower. When you are happy that you can produce a list of at least 15 meanings for any named combination of planet in sign, planet in house, or planet and planet, there are a couple of refinements to add. The nature of aspects has so far been ignored, but it must be allowed for, in two ways:

1) When interpreting an aspect, we must mainly be concerned with combining the nature of the two planets involved in it, but tradition also classifies aspects as "good" (trines and sextiles), "neutral" (conjunctions) and "bad" (most others).

2) When interpreting a planet in a sign or house (especially a sign), tradition provides alternative interpretations for "benaspected" or "malaspected" planets, not to mention planets which are neither. A "benasp." planet is one which receives mainly "good" aspects, and a "malasp." planet receives mainly "bad" aspects.

Do you detect out-of-date attitudes here? Modern astrology tries to avoid the good/bad distinction where aspects are concerned, preferring terms such as easy/difficult, soft/hard or passive/active. One might even say that there are no good or bad aspects in astrology, only good or bad people – if that weren't itself a dangerous oversimplification. Nevertheless it does seem to be true that when a planet receives mainly hard aspects, the native will find difficulty, at the least, in using the energies of that planet. It will mean effort on his part to overcome problems raised by the uneasy workings of the planet, and that effort may not always be rewarded by success, hence a possibility of falling into various faults such as bad temper, aggressiveness or dishonesty. But such traits cannot be assumed because of hard aspects, only suspected or warned against. Likewise the trines and sextiles will not guarantee success and happiness, only provide ease if the native can use them wisely.

So nothing is automatic in interpreting aspects, nor in taking account of the general state of a planet in a sign. The best approach in all cases is to be aware of ALL possible interpretations of the factor in question, but to lean towards the appropriate side. Let me clarify. Here are three interpretations for Sun in Capricorn:

1) Reliable, efficient and hardworking;
2) Cautious and painstaking;

3) Inhibited and unsociable.

These may fairly be described as good, neutral and bad meanings respectively. We need to take the view that all three are possible for ANY person with Sun in Capricorn, but if the Sun is "well-aspected" (mainly soft aspects) then 1) is much more likely than 3), and if the Sun is "afflicted" (misleading word!) then 3) is more likely than 1). With neutral or balanced aspects, 1) and 3) would be equally likely (or unlikely, whichever way you look at it). In all cases, 2) would be sure to apply. But as these are all "likelihoods", what do we settle for? As ever, *all* of them, but we need to make a note of the most, and least, likely meanings as we go.

Similarly with aspects. Apply all possible meanings, but bear likely trends in mind. Here a warning may be needed by inexperienced astrologers, particularly about hard aspects. Older books overstressed their "obstacle-making" nature, particularly with the square, and overlooked the dynamic, energy-forcing instability that these aspects provide. (There may be even more energy in semisquares.) Thus a common interpretation I used to get from students for Venus square Jupiter was "Can't show love", whereas it actually means "Can't stop showing love". When asked for their reasoning, these students invariably replied that the square would block the expression of love, and were surprised to hear me say that it really stimulated it. "Only Saturn blocks", I would say, and they were even more surprised to hear that Venus trine Saturn could mean "Can't show love". So, just to be clear, here are the principles:

1) The main core of any aspect meaning is to be found by combining the two planet meanings. (So Jupiter always expands and permits, Saturn always restricts and forbids).

2) The *way* in which the combined energies work out is shown by the nature of the aspect: easy aspects with ease, hard aspects with a compulsive, perhaps overdone and therefore clumsy, effort.

Just another couple of examples to clarify: Jupiter trine Uranus = "Able to achieve breakthroughs": Jupiter square Uranus = "Must achieve breakthroughs, even if they are messy ones". And remember that Mercury-square-Jupiter people are just as likely to be broadminded as Mercury-trine-Jupiter people. Perhaps more so.

Conjunctions seem to mean a combination of hard and soft. The person has an ability which is both easy and compulsive. In fact, it is as natural as breathing to him.

MODIFYING THE MEANINGS
It should be clear, then, that before we interpret a planet in a sign, we should take a look at its aspects to see whether hard or soft predominate – or whether there is a reasonable balance. This will influence our "grid" meanings. So if our former Moon in Taurus had been "malasp" we would have stretched out, or emphasised, the meanings concerned with being slow and boring; but had it been "benasp" we could have scratched out a few more meanings concerned with habits being reliable and practical rather than stodgy or unimaginative. It's really a kind of consciously-applied bias. It should also be clear that similar considerations apply when interpreting an aspect.

Again, as an exercise you would benefit from attempting to interpret some isolated planets or aspects, having regard to the nature of the aspects.

UNASPECTED PLANETS
Lack of aspects can be almost as revealing as their presence. For example a person with unaspected Saturn may have problems in exercising control in its various forms. This does *not* mean that his Saturn is necessarily weak, or that he is unable to control himself. As I shall show later, aspects derive their strength (partly) from planets, not vice versa. A person with an unaspected Saturn on the Ascendant has a strong Saturn to work with. But how will it work? In the manner of

the sign it occupies, of course; but obviously not through so many channels as planets having aspects: its influence will not so easily spread through the full interpretation: after all, it gets only one crack of the whip in our method as described so far, not five or six as other planets may do.

A useful metaphor is to think of the planets which aspect each other as being on the phone, though with direct lines rather than through an exchange. Those on the phone together can "talk" to each other and so find ways of working together. The stronger the aspect, the better the communication and so, potentially, the more obvious the working together. A Grand Cross or other configuration involves several planets all in mutual communication. But the unaspected planet has no one to discuss things with, and so must work on its own – therefore less predictably and less efficiently. But it will still work! So our hypothetical Saturn on the Ascendant will mean a person who can use control – but it will not be easy to say in what directions, or when. (The latter can be better defined by transits, no doubt.) Geoffrey Dean has described the workings of such planets in "all-or-nothing" terms, e.g. the person is highly controlled one minute, uncontrolled the next.

In reality, no planet is ever unaspected (in fact, every planet is aspected to every other) if we use more than the conventional aspects. By including not only quintiles, septiles, noviles, etc. but by continuing the "harmonics" upwards (dividing the circle by 10, 11, 12, 13 etc. to form different arcs) then sooner or later we are bound to find an aspect, even if we do not know what it means. A planet receiving none of the conventional aspects is simply receiving unconventional ones, the effects of which are more subtle and probably work at unconscious levels. One day perhaps we may understand all this – things are certainly moving in that direction.

Meanwhile, how do we construct an aspect grid or ladder for an unaspected planet? Regrettably, we are, at present, obliged to use only one keyword, "Unpredictable" against all the planet's keywords. But it had best be done if a complete picture of the native is to emerge.

It is also thought that two planets aspected only to each other behave as allies which always work together, but as unpredictably as a single planet.

The reality of unaspected or weakly aspected planets is probably concerned with personal integration, i.e. the properties of the planet are poorly integrated into the total personality. So a much-aspected planet is not thereby made *stronger*, but better integrated. A planet may be strong or weak, well integrated or poorly integrated, in any combination, not to mention average in either respect.

CHAPTER 4

SYNTHESIS (1): SIFTING THE BITS

NOTES AT THE READY
Before we can continue, I must assume that you have reached a stage in your work where you have in front of you numerous brief notes, representing the various interpretations of the various chart factors. I suggested that 15 meanings per factor is a good figure to aim at. Of course, results are bound to vary from chart to chart, but assuming a minimum of 24 chart factors (Ascendant and planets Sun – Saturn by sign, and about 16 aspects) this gives roughly 24 x 15 = 360 comments. If you use houses, another 150 comments. If you use other things, then even more. Allowing for the eventual disappearance of some remarks, there could still be *at least* 300 comments which are capable of expansion into meaningful sentences or even paragraphs.

Surprised? Well, I would be surprised, too, if you could come up with quite as many as that, for the simple reason that it is not easy actually to achieve 15 different meanings per factor, consistently. So let's settle for, oh... half that number. We have, then, about 130 remarks to work with. Much less and you haven't really been trying, at the analysis stage. Well, Margaret Hone did say it would take *work!* (With the theoretical target of 10 keywords per factor, the maximum would be about 2600.)

ORDER, ORDER!
Your notes, if you have followed my earlier advice, were written as the outcome of taking one chart factor at a time and extracting as many meanings from it as possible: therefore at

present they are grouped under the name of the chart factor (it is a good idea to keep these headings). Thus you might have:

Ascendant Libra
Meaning 1
Meaning 2
....
Meaning 10

Sun in Cancer
Meaning 1
....
Meaning 18

Moon in Gemini
(1-14)
And so on down to:

Neptune sextile Pluto
(1-4)

(Of course these numbers are hypothetical examples and are not to be taken literally.)

And here we come to the first of the Great Student Faults (as we may call them): writing a Final Report which reflects the order in which the Notes happened to be written down in the first place. Because they are misguided, bewildered, or just plain lazy, students very often drift into expanding the Notes into sentences, just as they come. The result is not only chaotic and difficult to follow, but will probably commit the next two Great Student Faults: 1) repeat itself sooner or later, and 2) (worse) contradict itself in different places.

The solution is to have a plan ready; one which suits a Final Report rather than the Notes; one indeed which the client can read and understand, also refer to later to confirm or clarify a particular point. In short, one which is arranged in order of topic rather than of planet. Again Hone has given us a blueprint: have a standard series of headings under which these topics can be grouped. She gives:

1) General Characteristics
2) Mentality, creativity.
3) Career, money, working ability.
4) Spare time occupations.
5) Personal contacts (friends, marriage).
6) Family contacts
7) Health
8) Travel

These are useful, though I myself use the following plan:

1) General Character
2) Mentality and Communications
3) Recreations and career
4) Social relationships
5) Love and marriage
6) Domestic and other matters
7) Life attitude

which is not very different. You can of course have your own plan, but it should reflect some thought on your part, and you should feel happy with it. My own scheme is also (mainly in my mind) subdivided within each category: I shall make this clear a little later. Although no scheme should be inflexible, it pays to start with the intention of sticking to the 7 or 8 headings you decide on. These headings will actually appear in the Final Report, by the way.

SORT, AND SORT AGAIN

But how do we get our Notes into the right order, ready for the final write-up? Hone gives us a hint here, but it is not nearly enough: "Abbreviations for (categories) are placed in the margins for easy collecting.... For final writing, the student must take the first category as decided and go through the notes on it only, selecting as the abbreviations indicate.... Each must be taken in turn in the same way, until all is welded into one whole." True, but there is much to do between the first and last of these operations. Having marked a category abbreviation in the margin against every comment, even when we collect up the first category, there are two more crucial operations: 1) Sort the Notes into the best order, *within* the category; 2) Balance, weigh, blend all those comments which relate to the same trait, and write *one* final comment reflecting your considered judgement on that trait. This last process is, of course, true synthesis, and it can only be accomplished efficiently if the previous stage, sorting, is properly achieved.

I cannot over-emphasise the importance of this second, inner sorting of notes. Without it, so much labour can be in vain, and so many false judgements perpetrated. It is hardly possible to do what Hone seems to be implying, that is to go through the notes extracting the relevant category and writing the Final Report direct from this. In practice one needs an intermediate document: sorted notes. How does one get this document into being? One of my students actually tried cutting the notes into pieces (with scissors), laying the strips around in an attempt to get a whole picture. Although this physical cutting-up may seem rather desperate, even crazy, it is in fact a correct way to get results, and its only real drawback is the difficulty of handling the pieces of paper (not to mention the disastrous possibility of a sudden draught). What we need is the equivalent of this physical re-sorting, but without the drawbacks.

There is nothing for it but more work. Make your intermediate sheet of notes under category headings, as they come, then look carefully at one category at a time. Decide in what order these notes belong. Mark a 1 against the first comment you will use, a 2 against the second, and so on. Then when the Final report is to be written up, your eye will alight on 1, 2 etc. in the correct order. If you feel you will be unable to do this, you might even be prepared to write yet another document (sorted notes) in which all remarks appear in the correct final order. So that we will have:

1) Original Notes (in order of planets, etc)
2) Categorised Notes (under category headings, but still in planetary order within each category.)
3) Sorted Notes (in which everything is in the right order)
4) Final Report (a greatly expanded version of 3)

Here's a brief (incomplete) example, taken from an actual piece of work: (I give only the first part of each document, to keep things simple.) The code letter on the left of each comment refers to the category heading, as above, and the number on the right refers to the strength of its chart source. This will all be explained later.

ORIGINAL NOTES

Sun Aquarius, malasp. (15)
S Likes company
L Platonic relationships
S Humanitarian
S Impersonal sympathy
C Determined, stubborn
M Annoyed when others don't understand
M Argumentative

Moon Gemini, malasp. (28)
C Moody, changeable
M Quick-witted
M Talkative
C Rationalises emotions
C Restless
D Frequent change of residence?
J Many short journeys
C Nervous, fidgety
R Too many interests
M Superficial

CATEGORISED NOTES

Character

20	**Determined, stubborn**	**15**
14	**Restless**	**28**
16	Methodical – sometimes	11
17	Realistic – sometimes	11
15	Adventurous	17
19	Patient adherence to principle	20
18	Discipline, rigidity	23
22	Irrational impulsiveness	11
21	Self-indulgent habits	10
23	Generous impulses	19
10	Sensitive	8
11	Energy, zeal	17
24	Secret actions	2
12	Showing energy versus trying to be controlled	26
13	Ruthless self-driving	23
5	**Moody, changeable**	**28**
9	Rationalises emotions	6
6	Volatile emotions	41
7	Short temper	2
8	Brings emotions to surface	6
4	Magnetism	3
2	Dramatic manner	32
1	**Nervous, fidgety**	**28**
3	Larger than life image (actor?)	17

Mentality

1	**Quick witted**	**28**
4	**Superficial**	**28**
7	Good concentration -sometimes	11
5	Broad understanding	4
6	Superstition/dogma?	15
2	Impressionable	7
3	Liable to confusion	12

10	Self-confident	16
8	Fertile imagination	12
9	Dream World	12
12	Loves to utter thoughts of universal significance	15
13	Inspired by romantic thoughts	7
11	Intellectually complacent	15

(and 14 other comments under Mentality)

SORTED NOTES

Character

Nervous, Fidgety	**28**
Dramatic manner	32
Larger than life image (actor?)	17
Magnetism	3
Moody, changeable	**28**
Volatile emotions	41
Short temper	2
Brings emotions to surface	6
Rationalises emotions	6
Sensitive	8
Energy, zeal	17
Showing energy versus trying to be controlled	26
Ruthless self-driving	23
Restless	**28**
Adventurous	17
Methodical – sometimes	11
Realistic – sometimes	11
Discipline, rigidity	23
Patient adherence to principle	20
Determined, stubborn	**15**
Self-indulgent habits	10
Irrational impulsiveness	11
Generous impulses	19
Secret actions	2

Mentality

Quick-witted	**28**

Impressionable	7
Liable to confusion	12
Superficial	**28**
Broad understanding	4
Superstition/dogma?	15
Good concentration – sometimes	11
Fertile imagination	12
Dream world	12
Self-confident	16
Intellectually complacent	15
Loves to utter thoughts of universal significance	15
Inspired by romantic thoughts	7

(And 14 other comments under Mentality)

The above must be studied carefully if you are to understand what is going on. Please note the following considerations:
1) To save confusion by too much detail, only the first two sections of each document are given, and even then the Mentality section is only half-complete. This does not matter provided that the principles are understood.
2) Many of the remarks in the Original Notes do not appear again, because we are only showing the General Character (C) and Mentality (M) categories. Likewise, many comments appear in the Categorised Notes and Sorted Notes which did not derive from Sun and Moon signs. To help you trace those remarks that are found in all three sets of Notes, we have printed them in bold type.
3) In the Original Notes, category letters are usually put into the lefthand margin after all the notes have been written: though there is no reason why you should not put them in as you go along, if you prefer it. However, in the Categorised Notes, the numbers in the left-hand margin (representing the eventual order of the remarks) can only be entered AFTER all the notes have been grouped into categories.
4) It is not normally too difficult to decide in which category a remark belongs. But the sorting within each category must be done with the utmost care; the order represented by the

numbers in the above example is not just an arbitrary preference, it embodies two important principles. First, subdividing the categories into (unnamed) lesser categories. Read the Sorted Notes carefully. Do you see that the first four remarks constitute an unheaded subcategory "General impression given to others"? And that the next six remarks deal with the emotions? The following five comments deal with the native's general approach to life, and the last six his methodology. There is no set pattern for these subdivisions, for they will vary from chart to chart, but they should be created, so that similar topics come together, to make a more logical Final Report; one that does not wander from topic to topic and back. Second, the sorting must be done in such a way that any remarks dealing with the *same* or *opposite* principles are brought together, side by side, for your evaluation. *This is one of the main conditions for proper synthesis*. Thus notice how the method brought together:

> Moody, changeable
> Volatile emotions

which say the same thing, and:

> Energy, zeal
> Showing energy versus trying to be controlled
> Ruthless self-driving

which deal with two sides of a problem.
Then again, we have:

> Discipline, rigidity
> Patient adherence to principle
> Determined, stubborn

which all tell the same story, but immediately following we see:

> Self-indulgent habits
> Irrational impulsiveness
> Generous impulses

which are virtually opposite. Synthesis can only be achieved when such grouping has taken place, whether mentally or on paper—and I advise paper. (I will elaborate on how we judge the final outcome in the next chapter: meanwhile we are concerned with organising our notes.)

STREAMLINING THE PROCESS

Working exactly as above, but in full, i.e. writing our hundreds of remarks no less than three times before even thinking about the Final Report, is certainly a very daunting prospect! (Though one that I have personally done many times.) Can we shorten the process at all? One answer is to keep the remarks as short as possible, and to use abbreviations—provided you know what they stand for. So, for example, I sometimes write "emot conf" to stand for "emotional confusion" and "ma-fix" to mean "mother-fixation": just use whatever code you will be happy with.

Another possibility is to omit the Sorted Notes (I mentioned this earlier), and do the sorting mentally when you are preparing the Final Report. But this is dangerous unless you are a very careful person, and I certainly recommend beginners to do several charts fully, as described above, before attempting this shortcut.

I am as human as anybody; and, looking for an easier method, and being lucky enough to have a computer with printer, managed to write a computer program which does all the sorting for me. I only need to type in my remarks once, with category-letters prefixed, and the computer will sort into categories, and again re-sort into the precise order I want within each category. I have to do a little intermediate responding to the computer, but I don't have to retype the remarks: at the end of the process the computer has printed out my original remarks in final sorted order.

Failing a computer, the only way to reshuffle remarks after writing them only once would seem to be the scissor-method adopted by the desperate student! But there may be other ways you might think of... Whatever method you do adopt, make absolutely sure that it brings together all remarks that belong together, in any of these three important ways:

1) They refer to the same trait.
2) They refer to opposite traits.
3) They are on a similar topic.

Once your notes are correctly sorted to the best of your ability, you are ready for final synthesis.

CATEGORY SUBDIVISIONS
In the Appendix I give the particular way I tend to subdivide my categories, to show the kind of thing that makes work even more systematic. By all means disregard it and use your own scheme: my way suits me but may not suit everybody: however as an example it may be of some value. In any case, I am always prepared to depart from it if a particular chart seems to call for different treatment.

No one can complain of shortage of ideas with this plan before them: I count some 200 traits, most of which have unstated opposites which I am sure you can reconstruct easily.

These subdivision headings do not appear in my reports. I am conscious of them, and normally take them in the order given, allowing for the flexibility just mentioned. It is a good idea to make one paragraph out of each subheading: that way, although the reader does not see the subheadings, he is made aware of them in a subtle way.

Have this plan by you when you write up your final Report. Of course you can depart from it as soon as you feel confident you have found something better, but it is best to have some sort of pre-arranged plan ready at all stages of your development. I myself depart frequently from my own plan as I come across a chart which requires something to be added or omitted.

CHAPTER 5

SYNTHESIS (2): EVALUATION

Now we are ready for the stage requiring most judgement, experience, wisdom and nerve! We have all the bits and pieces in front of us, and we are ready to form ultimate judgements about the person whose chart we are interpreting. The main problems at this stage are:

1) Resolving contradictions
2) Knowing what to emphasise
3) Knowing what to play down or even leave out.

The point is that, although in one sense our Sorted Notes are ready for expansion into the Final Report, in that everything is categorised and in the right order, we still have the problem of knowing what to do when several remarks (deriving from several different chart sources) bear on the same trait, or trait-pair of opposites like Impulsive/Cautious. This is the central problem of synthesis, in fact. It would seem fairly clear that when three or four chart factors have all agreed that the native is, say, impulsive, and nothing says that he is cautious, the outcome is impulsiveness. That's an easy one! But should we perhaps say he is "very impulsive" or, further, "excessively impulsive", or even "impulsive to the point of foolishness"? Maybe the ideal phrase is "slightly impulsive", in spite of four chart sources agreeing? Certainly one of the Great Student Faults is putting "very" or "tremendously" in front of almost everything, without any real justification. (Students, particularly in their early stages, get so excited with the power of astrology that they seem almost drunk at times!) We need, then, some guidance in the *degree* to which a person may be manifesting a trait.

But the problem of degree is not confined to those situations where several chart factors concur: even more of a quandary arises when one chart source suggests a trait and a different source suggests its opposite. (Or maybe several sources take sides, some pointing one way, some the other.) One might be forgiven for thinking that it is a matter of a simple vote count, e.g. "2 in favour of impulsive, 3 in favour of cautious; therefore he's cautious."; or "2 in favour of impulsive, 2 in favour of cautious, therefore it cancels out and he's neither." But the real solution to such problems has to be found, not merely by a headcount of chart sources, but by a careful consideration of how strong each influence is. It is quite common for 3 sources "voting" for a trait to be easily outweighed by a strong single source "voting" in the opposite direction.

STRENGTH OF CHART FACTORS

So we need some method of evaluating the strength of each and every chart factor that we are using. It is fatal to treat everything alike! This particularly applies to aspects: another common Great Student Fault (we'll make a list of these before long) is to notice whether an aspect is within orb *or not*, and to interpret one that is barely within orb equally with an exact aspect. In other words "Sun square Mars is Sun square Mars and there's an end of it." But virtually all good astrologers are agreed that the closer the aspect, the stronger the influence, and this can only mean that the strength gradually fades as we look at wider and wider orbs, till at the threshold of the widest permitted orb, the influence is so faint that we may as well ignore it. So if we take 8 degrees as our maximum for a square, then a square of orb 7 degrees 55 minutes is virtually the same as a non-existent square, *not* the same as a square of orb 0 degrees 5 minutes. Some astrologers go further and regard an applying aspect as stronger than a separating one, though this principle is less well established.

STRENGTH OF PLANETS

But other principles are at work, too. There is such a thing as a strong or weak planet. Tradition has long taught that certain conditions strengthen a planet or make its operation more favourable, and one of the first jobs in chart interpretation should be a careful assessment of the relative strengths of the planets. A number of criteria have been suggested at various times:

1) Angularity (proximity to Ascendant, Descendant, MC, IC)
2) Placed in own sign (rulership)
3) Placed in sign of exaltation
4) Placed in house corresponding to sign rulership
5) Being the ruler of the Ascendant
6) Receiving a large number of aspects
7) Planetary hierarchy, i.e. Sun strongest by nature, down to Pluto as weakest.
8) Travelling at faster (or slower!) speed than average
9) Being nearer to the Earth (or Sun!) than average
10) Moving direct rather than retrograde (or vice versa!)
11) Being in certain of the "Moon's Mansions"

and there are probably others. It is for every astrologer to use whatever criteria he believes to be valid; though for myself, having tested them all, I am convinced that only the first of these criteria, namely angularity, can be demonstrated beyond reasonable doubt, though I also have a leaning, maybe irrationally, to 7). The most tempting of the others is perhaps 6); but we have only to reflect that on this rule an unaspected planet would be weaker, whereas there is plenty of evidence that an unaspected or "weakly" aspected planet can still have a strong effect, though it is not necessarily strong just by being unaspected. If it is weakly placed in the chart, *and* unaspected, then it will have very little effect on the person, at least in an obvious way. In my view, aspects receive strength from planets, not vice versa.

So, once we have evaluated the relative strengths of our

planets, we will be paying attention to this when we pass judgement on conflicting meanings. Thus if a weakly placed Mars says "This man is aggressive" and a strongly placed Venus says "He is placid", we would tend to believe Venus, other things being equal. But how do we keep track of the relative strengths? One answer is to use a points system, even though the allocation of these points is bound to be somewhat arbitrary. How *much* stronger is the strongest possible planet than the weakest? Here one can only guess, and I have experimented with various points systems, usually settling for one in which the strongest possible score is about 3 times the weakest possible. But for many purposes we need not try for a mathematically exact method: three levels (weak, normal, strong) are sufficient for most work; and it is easy to maintain this distinction in one's notes by using three different colour pens, or by putting comments for weak sources in brackets and underlining those for strong ones.

STRENGTH OF ASPECTS

Just as there is probably a natural hierarchy among the planets, from Sun down to Pluto (over and above other criteria) so there is probably a natural hierarchy among aspects, from conjunction down to semisextile/quincunx, or whatever is the smallest aspect we use. N.B. by "smallest" I do not mean literally the smallest arc (say 30 degrees) but the largest number we are dividing the circle by. E.g. for a square we are dividing the circle by 4, for semisquares *and* sesqui-squares by 8 (so these two are equal in the hierarchy) and for semisextile *and* quincunx we are dealing with 12ths of a circle. So other things being equal, a conjunction is stronger than an opposition, a sextile is stronger than a semisquare, and so on.

But other things never are equal. First of all we have to take regard of how close the actual orb is (the closer the stronger) and then we need to know how strong are the two planets comprising the aspect. The strength of the aspect is a combination of:

1) Strength of the two planets
2) Hierarchy of the aspect types
3) Closeness of the actual orb

It may not always be easy to compare the strength of one aspect with another (for example, is a close sextile between two weak planets stronger than a loose conjunction between one strong and one weaker planet?) Again some kind of points system should be helpful, if you are mathematically minded: if you are not, you will simply have to form an estimate of the strength of each aspect. But make no mistake, *the attempt must be made somehow*. As mentioned earlier, it may be sufficient to recognise three levels (weak, normal, strong) though I do feel there is far more room for variation with aspects than with planets, so perhaps five levels would be more appropriate.

JUDGING THE TRAITS

THE PROBLEM

We come at last to the actual process of forming judgements as to whether, and to what degree, a particular meaning will apply to the native whose chart we are interpreting. For convenience I refer to these meanings as traits, even though a few of them may be better described by some other word. Many of these traits go in opposing pairs, as we have already seen; and these are the ones likely to give us problems in forming final judgements; others have no opposite, and are either possessed by the native or they are not (for example artistic ability).

In the latter cases the first problem is to decide whether there is sufficient evidence to warrant a remark at all, or to omit reference to this trait on the grounds that chart influences are too weak. If there is sufficient influence, the second problem is the degree to which this is manifesting. Do we say, for example, "You have artistic talent", or "You are artistic above average", or "You have enormous talent in art, and are bound to succeed and become famous"? (Much more likely, we should be saying "You have a mild liking for art", for one of the weaknesses of astrology itself is to infer too much from Venus in a chart, almost from its mere presence. More of this later.)

In the case of opposing trait-pairs we have the same two problems, but twice over, of course, not to mention the question of deciding which side wins.

What is the best method of making these judgements? There can be no firm answer to this question, but since this book is intended to be helpful I will suggest three ways of going about it:

1) Use a points-scoring system, and decide on the basis of fixed thresholds.
2) Use a few simple strength levels, and decide the outcome by commonsense evaluation.
3) Estimate strengths and make decisions based on experience.

I will elaborate a little on each method.

POINTS SYSTEM

In this, we begin by allocating a number of points to each planet, to represent its strength, on the principles outlined above. I would suggest an average of 20 points as a starting point, with fluctuations from 10 to 30 as extremes. The points for each planet would then be applied to each and every meaning derived from a) planet in sign; b) planet in house. (Though as houses are less important than signs you might consider using only half-strength for house interpretations.) Study page 32, where Sun is given 15 points and Moon 28; then page 33: see how these figures turn up every time the Sun or Moon remarks appear. A problem arises with points for the Ascendant (and MC if you use it) when interpreting by sign. I prefer to give Ascendant a fixed score of 20, but if you believe its strength is affected by the aspects it receives, or by the strength of its ruler, then you would modify this figure accordingly.

The aspects would then be allocated points based partly on these strengths, as implied above. My own formula for aspect strength takes care of the aspect hierarchy by first assuming orbs on a sliding scale:

Conjunction	8 degrees
Opposition	7
Trine	6
Square	5
Sextile	4
Semisquare, sesquisquare	3
Semisextile, quincunx	2

Simple to remember, and though it is a compromise between old and new (harmonic) systems, it produces good results. Now the formula can be applied:

Aspect strength = (P1 + P2) x (M − A) / M

where P1 = strength of planet 1
       P2 = strength of planet 2
       M   = maximum orb allowed
       A   = actual orb

All this does is to add up the strengths of the two planets and take a proportion of this depending on the actual orb and allowing for the hierarchy of aspects. It may surprise you to realise that this makes, for example, a sextile of orb 1 degree exactly as powerful as a conjunction of 4 degrees orb; or an *exact* semisextile as powerful as an *exact* conjunction. This is in line with modern thinking.

Results will show wide fluctuations, from 1 point up to say 70. But the matter is complicated by the fact that some charts yield many more aspects than others. I think a reasonable view is to ensure that the *total* points used in in interpreting signs/houses should equal the *total* points used in interpreting aspects. This unfortunately involves some preliminary checking and adjusting, and to go this far makes an already complicated system more complicated. In fact, this kind of accuracy is better suited to a computer. However, since more and more astrologers are using computers and calculators, there will always be some people who are prepared to make such calculations. A useful alternative to this is to assume, say, 16 as the average number of aspects (this will be true if you use the above scale of orbs) and count the number of aspects in the chart in question. Call this NA and the formula now is:

Aspect strength = $(P1 + P2) \times (M - A) / M \times (16 / NA)$

Make a list of all strengths, whether planet or aspect and have it handy when the judgemental stage is reached. Calculations, either exact or approximate, can then be made by looking up the strength of each influence (assuming you can remember, that is, which planet or aspect the influence originated from.) If your memory is poor, you will have to mark these strengths against each meaning in the sorting stage. See the numbers to the right of the meanings on pages 33 to 35. Here's an example (taken from page 34) to show how the final calculations would work out:

Discipline, rigidity	23
Patient adherence to principle	20
Determined, stubborn	15
	——
	58
Self-indulgent habits	10
Irrational impulsiveness	11
Generous impulses	19
	——
	40

This is a majority of 18 points for the first group, but because the opposite group have a respectable total I would allow the losers some say, thus:

"You have a firm respect for discipline and approve of

keeping rules wherever possible. In your own activities you try to keep your sights on what you are aiming at, and would not be easily deflected from your purpose. Nevertheless there can be moments when you give way to an irrational impulse, or break rules to suit yourself or to please others."

But not everyone would count the remark "Generous impulses" as relevant to the Disciplined/Undisciplied question. If you feel that way, then clearly the scoring is quite different (58 against 21), and no remark at all need be made about lack of discipline. (Omit the words from "Nevertheless" onwards in the above.) However, some separate remark about the generous impulses would now be needed.

SIMPLE EVALUATION
For planets, have three levels of strength; for aspects, five. Devise your own way of marking these, by coloured inks or underlinings, etc. Either a) have a master list as in the points method above, or b) maintain these markings throughout the various stages of notes. Using the example from the previous chapter (page 32) suppose that Sun in Aquarius is considered weak, and that you are using brackets to indicate this, then all the Sun meanings (Likes company and so on) would be enclosed in brackets, on all three of the Notes sheets. Thus in judging the final groups (eg. Discipline, rigidity etc as on page 36) you would notice which traits were weak and which were strong. "Determined, stubborn" would appear in brackets, whereas "Irrational impulsiveness" might be marked as strong, by underlining.

ESTIMATION
Should only be attempted after you have a fair amount of experience. No scores or markings of any kind are written down, but the relative strengths of all chart factors are *estimated* and either remembered or re-estimated by glancing at the birthchart, when forming the final judgements. This kind of practised judgement is often referred to as intuition,

which is quite the wrong word. Notice that we are not guessing, or going by "feel", we are in effect using scores and strength levels just as in the two previous methods, but they are blurred rather than exact; judged rather than measured. Personally I find the following procedure very helpful when using this approach. Make all the notes that are necessary, up to the point of beginning the final judgements. Ponder all these notes, forming preliminary mental judgements but writing nothing down. Try to visualise the person in the horoscope, standing in front of you, moving, talking, behaving. (Very often the person I visualise at this stage does not "add up" or "make sense" – there are too many oddities or contradictions.) *go to bed*, i.e. sleep on it, and only write up the Final Report next day, when your subconscious has had a chance to work. I always find that the contradictions have become reconciled, the oddities have fallen into focus, and I can see a person in whose existence I can actually believe. Now is the time to write about him, whereas yesterday I would have produced a distorted or unbelievable picture.

MAKING THE ACTUAL JUDGEMENT

Whatever method you use to help you assemble the evidence, the principles guiding the actual judgement are the same. In fact, having used the words "judgement" and "evidence" I may as well pursue the metaphor and liken the process to a trial – perhaps like the Judgement of Solomon ("To which mother shall I award the baby, this one, that one, or neither? Or do I divide equally?") And it is almost literally a matter of hearing the evidence for both sides and deciding which has put up the stronger case. But perhaps an even more useful metaphor is that of a vote after a debate, for (certainly when using a scoring system) we can actually count the votes (N.B. votes, not voters) by seeing how many points are in favour of Caution and how many are in favour of Impulse, for example. But it is not quite so simple as saying "Caution got the most votes, so he is a cautious man". Much depends on how big the majority is. Did Caution win by a crushing majority or by a narrow margin? And do we use the word "very" in our final phrase? Let's look at some possible situations and spell out what the decisions should be:

Caution pts	Impulse pts	Majority	Verdict
Few	None	Tiny	No remark
Few	Few	None	No remark
Several	None	Good	Cautious
Several	Few	Fair	Slightly cautious
Many	Several	Good	Cautious
Many	Few or none	Large	Very Cautious
Very many	Few or none	V large	Extremely cautious

This is all clear, I hope. Notice that nothing is said when the majority is small, *and* the total "vote" is small. But an entirely different situation arises when there are a large number of votes on both sides, ending with a small or non-existent majority. *Powerful contrary influences do not cancel out.* In such cases we have to accept that the native will manifest both the opposing traits, perhaps on different occasions, perhaps in some combination. So the next table shows some more situations:

Total pts	Caution majority	Verdict
Large	Appreciable	1) Cautious, some impulse
Large	Small or none	2) Both traits
Very large	Small to good	3) Both traits
Huge	Small to good	4) Both traits

(2), (3), and (4) are different types of deadlock. At the first, lowest level, we need to say that the person is somehow balanced between the two opposing traits. At the second level, because total influences are stronger, the person has more of a problem: he is "pulled" between them. At the third, very strong level, the problem is more severe: he is "torn" between them. We need to find sensible wordings for these situations: unfortunately it is impossible to make any rules for this, because everything depends on the traits and how they might be reconciled. Clearly a man can be cautious a lot of the time, and impulsive on certain occasions, so we could say "You have a cautious nature which generally prevails, but now and then you act on impulse": this is an example of how we might word the first situation in the above table. For (2) we might say "Caution and impulse seem equally a part of your nature", for (3) "Caution and impulse often seem to pull you in different directions", and for (4) "Caution and impulse seem perpetually at war in you". However, the wordings could well be totally different with another trait-pair such as Versatile/Specialist: a man is unlikely to be versatile on some occasions and a specialist on others. More likely he could prove versatile in some situations or departments of life, and a specialist in others; but possibly the most likely outcome is that he would be a specialist in several different subjects. (That does make sense the more you think about it.) Think out each of these "deadlock" situations very carefully and use commonsense to help you find the right wording.

THRESHOLDS
In the above two tables I used words such as "Good", "Huge" and "Tiny" to indicate vote-majorities, i.e. the final score for a particular trait, after deducting the score for the opposite trait. It is a good idea to have a fairly firm concept of those points where you are going to switch from one level to another. For example, what is the minimum score, below which you intend to say nothing? How much total strength do you want to see before you use the word "very"? Or "tremendous"? How many total votes do you want (on *both* sides) before you assess a balanced situation? Those using a points system will need to define these precisely: here's a suggested table, but don't take it on trust, try it out, for much depends how you work your scoring system in the first place: this also depends on how many chart factors you use, what your aspect orbs are, and so on. But some sort of guide is better than none:

Score	Verdict
Below 16	(Ignore)
16 – 25	"Slightly…"
25 – 70	(Normal)
70 – 100	"Very…"
Over 100	"Extremely…"

With the balanced traits, total points for both sides added together should be greater than 70, and majority for one side not more than 10. For "pulled", 150 and 20. For "torn", 300 and 40. Remember, these are only suggestions. In practice, the Final Report should not be larded with "very"s and "extremely"s; and there had better not be more than half a dozen of the balanced-type traits, if that. If there are, raise your threshold figures. On the other hand, if the word "very" never appears, you should consider lowering your threshold figures. Most people are very something or other, if only in one respect.

WHAT HAS BEEN ACHIEVED?

In an earlier chapter I advised the inclusion of *all* the possible meanings for each chart factor at the analysis stage, promising that things would get sorted out later. It has become clearer, I hope, how that works: meanings which appear only once, unsupported by other chart sources (unless from a strong source), are likely to end up with a low score and are thus likely to be excluded; and meanings that encounter their opposite are also unlikely to survive, provided we have set our thresholds properly. Whereas meanings from strong sources or those reinforced by several sources, will not only survive, but may even be prefixed by words such as "very" or "extremely". Remember, none of these "votes" and verdicts could have been arrived at unless we had correctly brought together those meanings which belong together, by being either part of the same trait or part of the opposite one: hence the vital importance of the two sorting processes in the Notes.

However, even then a few traits will slip through which should not, if we have been assiduous at the analysis stage. For example, a Venus-Uranus aspect should include the possibility of homosexuality, and that meaning (if you wish) could go down in the Original Notes for every chart in which you see such an aspect. But you are going to get into a lot of trouble if you go about telling all Venus-Uranus people they are homosexuals! Because this is one of the less likely meanings, it should not survive into the Final Report unless a) the aspect has a really huge score, such as it might accrue from an exact conjunction sitting on the Ascendant; or b) other chart sources agree with this, suggesting some degree of inability to sustain normal heterosexual relationships (even Sun square Moon would help here). On the other hand, there is little harm in suggesting to anyone with Venus-Uranus predominating that they might make and break relationships quickly. Notice that I said predominating. A good score from Venus-Saturn or Venus in Capricorn could make all the difference. But to return to my main point, I am saying that any dubious meanings which do not seem to fit into the overall character should be discarded if they originate from only one, moderately weak source. Thus our way of working takes care of those cook-book qualifications such as "provided the rest of the chart concurs", and we were able to take all meanings at their face value in the first instance, leaving final sifting to the stage when all strengths had been evaluated and all relevant issues brought together.

If we now miss an important feature, or let contradictions through, it is our own fault: we will at least have made the best possible preparations to favour correct and balanced judgements at every point in the Final Report. We have created the ideal conditions in which to begin writing sentences which will be read by a client, so we must now begin to address ourselves to that task.

CHAPTER 6

THE FINAL REPORT

We have, then, done all our preliminary chart erection, chart analysis, weightings of factors, three sets of notes, and some preliminary judgements about the outcome of trait-conflicts; and we are ready to write up the Final Report. We might perhaps be forgiven for feeling that by the time we have arrived at this point we are too exhausted to go any further... Well, as I indicated in the last chapter, it is in any case a good idea to "sleep on it" before attempting this final task, so, having done that, no excuses: there's more work to be done!

THE GREAT STUDENT FAULTS
Now is probably the best moment to tabulate all the Great Student Faults, so as to warn you against committing them. At least, all those I have come across – I daresay someone is capable of dreaming up a new one. Here they are, with explanations:

1) Report follows chart order instead of category order. This was referred to above (page 29): the student, having made notes direct from the chart, does not sort them; thus the result wanders from topic to topic and back, and is sure to commit errors 3) and 4) below. Anyone who had read this book up to here will be aware of the reasons why sorting is vital: and naturally sorting is aimed at creating a text in which each topic is dealt with once and for all, under headings which are a clear guide where to find a particular topic.

2) Remarks in the wrong category. E.g. references to Social Relationships in the General Character. This is all too easily done, for example with Argumentativeness. But you cannot

argue on your own; it does properly belong under Social Relationships, so wait till you get there! General Character, being the first category, usually suffers most from this error: it should contain only those traits which are not better dealt with elsewhere; these must be general in character (as the heading suggests!) and should give a fair picture of the person, *before* he sets about any particular activity. The cure for this error is to take more care when labelling remarks with the category code letters.

3) Repeating oneself. This can only be expected to happen if note-sorting has been inadequate or omitted, since one object of the sorting is to bring all repetitions together for judgement. So if Sun in Gemini, Moon in Sagittarius, and Moon opposite Jupiter all suggest lack of concentration, we should tell the client this once, not three times in three different places. There is normally no excuse for repetition, for it should be picked up when re-reading the script: however I have seen many cases where it has been done deliberately, for we read "As I said before..." Is the student desperate to fill space? Does he think that the slow-witted client has forgotten? Is he repeating himself for the sake of emphasis? The only time I feel repetition is permissible is where fresh light is being thrown: for example if under "Mentality" I had written "Your memory is not too reliable, and this may let you down when it comes to study", I might later invoke the bad memory with reference to Social Relationships, as "Sometimes you unwittingly offend people by nothing worse than forgetting their name or getting the time of a meeting wrong. Your bad memory will need countering by charm if you are to even the score." But notice that I say "Your bad memory", implying that the reader has already seen this; I do not say "You have a bad memory" at this point, as if it were a piece of news, and I even prefer to avoid "As I said before, you have a bad memory."

4) Contradicting oneself. (Possibly the most widespread of all faults.) This very seldom consists of an immediate contradic-

tion, rather of two conflicting statements on different pages. Again the lack of proper remark-sorting is probably to blame; but again it *should* be picked up by the astrologer re-reading the script when it is complete. If such discrepancies are not noticed then the astrologer has a bad memory as well as a bad method! To put the matter baldly, if you contradict yourself you have not performed synthesis, and you are expecting the client to perform it for you.

5) Overstressing traits. In a nutshell, over-use of words like "very", "extremely", "tremendously". Not only students are prone to this: I have heard astrologers who should know better larding their lectures with these words. If I believed all I have heard, virtually everything in the chart has a "tremendous" effect on us. No wonder the scientific community look askance at astrology if at the same time as we display this naive enthusiasm we are unable to prove anything. If Sun in Leo makes us "tremendously creative" it should be easy to prove this by statistics. But of course it isn't like that: it is only one chart in twenty or thirty that has anything tremendous in it at all. Save the "very"s, then when you do use them, they will be all the more effective. An orchestra should not play fortissimo all the time!

6) Too readily giving the native a dual personality. Fascinated by the number of balanced traits they encounter, some students delight in telling their client that he has a dual or even a split personality; possibly even going so far as to invoke Jekyll and Hyde. They should reflect that we are all subject to conflicting influences and opposing desires: it is perfectly normal. Only in a very extreme case should it be necessary to make an issue of it.

7) Ignoring weightings. In other words, not bothering to distinguish between strong and weak planets or aspects. This makes synthesis harder rather than easier. The commonest and worst version of this fault is to treat all aspects alike, regardless of orb, etc., and the next most common is to treat

dubious chart entities like the Part of Fortune or the cuspal rulership of an empty house as if they were on a par with Sun or Moon sign.

8) Using technical terms. "Your Mars in Scorpio makes you very sexy." (If I were very sexy I would prefer to be told just that, not that a planet out in space "made" me so.) (By the way, did you notice how the "very" slipped in again?) Margaret Hone rightly advises us not to use astrological terms in our reports, other than perhaps very generally on the front cover, since many people want to know at least their Sun, Moon and Ascendant signs). It should be easy enough for us all to resolve to exclude all astrological terms from the main body of the report. But a more insidious jargon is that of psychology, and many students love talking about egos and complexes and the unconscious when they hardly know the meaning of these terms. Such words can be used, but only with some care, and then only when there is no better way to make things clear, for the client may not understand the jargon. Too many astrologers act as pseudo-psychiatrists.

9) Using other people's phrases. This is jargon again, but instead of pure astrological terms, students use verbal phrases (associated with interpretation) which they have picked up, sometimes unconsciously, from astrology books. Alas, Hone herself is often involved: here are some of her oft-quoted phrases which flow awkwardly from the pens of other writers:

"Your nature, as seen from your chart..."
"Your real desires are towards...."
"Your whole tendency is towards..."
"The good things of the earth"
"...in—ways."

Little harm is done, perhaps, but it is far better for a student to develop his own literary style. However, such literal copying from other sources can have a worse effect: "You seek to scoop up from experience and give to your fellows, either constructively or vindictively." (From M.E. Jones' explanation of the "Bowl Shape". I have no idea what this curious phrase "scoop up from experience" means, and I have never met anyone who can explain it. Clearly the student doesn't understand either, but he feels he has to write it, and he has no idea how to translate it into English. Even when apparently concocting their own phrases, students can run into trouble if using keywords too literally. I once read the following: "Your nebulousness will be expressed with precision" (for Neptune in Virgo!) What on earth does such a sentence mean? Even if it didn't contradict itself, the semi-astrological jargon involved is enough to make it a puzzle to the reader. My advice is, *always* use your own words: at least you will know what you meant, and can defend your meaning.

10) Being too vague or doubtful. As the last example shows, the reader should not be set puzzles. Sometimes, either out of a misguided attempt to be tactful, or perhaps through getting carried away with his own verbosity, a student writes something like "In certain situations you might find it to your advantage to consider whether a change of plan might not be beneficial in the long run, bearing in mind all the factors involved". I think the student is trying to say "Be flexible." But I'm not sure, there are so many ifs and buts:

"In certain situations..." We can't take this as a definite statement, then.
"... you might..." Even less definite.
"... consider whether.." More doubt.
"... a change of plan.." *what* change of plan?
"... might not be beneficial..." uncertain again.
"... in the long run". More hedging of bets.
"... bearing in mind all the factors involved." More qualification.

Most clients would shrug off a sentence like this as a virtual non-statement.

11) Being too blunt or positive. "Your marriage will end on

the rocks." (Venus-Uranus rearing its ugly head again, or perhaps Uranus in the 7th house?) Does the writer *know* that the marriage is doomed? Of course an experienced astrologer shrinks from making such positive announcements, or (if he must make them) making them in such a crude and potentially hurtful fashion. Apparently more innocuous is something such as "You will succeed in life." Very nice to be told that, but really astrology cannot be sure that a man will be successful (assuming we know what the man himself means by success). More moderately, we should say "You are likely to experience a high degree of success in your goals."

12) Failing to use quite the right word. Our language is so rich in synonyms, each with a different shade of meaning, that it is important to take a little trouble over the right wording. Look at these words: do they all mean the same? Thrifty, careful, parsimonious, mean, miserly. Clearly there is a gradual shift of meaning as we go through the list, even though all deal with spending money reluctantly. But a thrifty person will not welcome being told he is mean! Or: gregarious, sociable, society-loving, friendly, flirtatious, unfaithful, philandering, heart-breaker. These make a progression from totally harmless to totally destructive, yet all deal with the same basic human trait, in a general sense. It is important to pitch one's meaning at exactly the right level.

ASTROLOGICAL PITFALLS
Well, this goes far enough with student errors. We can forgive them, for the student will learn, and once he realises the pitfalls he can learn to avoid them. But astrology itself has pitfalls waiting for us: these are less easy to detect. It all comes about because astrology (traditional astrology anyway) seems rather fond of certain topics; much fonder than the man in the street would be, if he tried to analyse the character of his wife or friend. So if we are not careful, we may overemphasise these matters, or postulate them as traits when they don't really exist. Here they are:

1) Artistic nature. Almost any planet in Taurus, Libra or Pisces, and virtually any Venus aspect, all seem to bestow artistic ability or tastes on a person. Since it would be difficult to find a chart without a fair proportion of the foregoing, virtually everybody is artistic (or musical)! Clearly we must guard against judging anyone to be an artist, especially by career, unless the sources combine to give an unusually high score in this direction. If in doubt, play it down. Better still, always play it down.

2) Philosophy, Religion, Travel. The minute you get anything in Sagittarius or the 9th house, or if Jupiter so much as blinks, you are going to be told by most textbooks that you are involved in these things. Again that goes for all of us!
Wait for an unusually high score before abandoning caution and saying "You have an interest in philosophy and religion". Most people either don't have this interest, or if they do, they take it for granted and wouldn't think it worth the astrologer's while to point it out.

3) Prisons, hospitals and similar institutions. "Have you, dear client, got anything in your 12th house? Then I am forced to tell you that you will be involved with prisons, hospitals, and similar institutions." Is it any wonder that many people reject astrology when we make such crude rules for ourselves? As a simple exercise, work out the odds in favour of having at least one planet, or a node, in the 12th house.

4) Legacies. Need I go on? It only takes one planet in the 8th....

5) Psychic ability. Once again, astrology is ready, at the drop of a hat, to tell you that you are psychic, intuitive, or even telepathic and clairvoyant. You won't need much, just an aspect to Neptune, or a planet or two in Pisces or the 12th house...

6) The occult, or astrology. With almost any aspect to Uranus or Neptune, or both, plus some other things, perhaps, you are a potential astrologer. Again, few charts lack something on

these lines, but not one person in 10,000 is actually an astrologer. Best if we only tell a very few people they have this ability.

7) Health. I am very far from being convinced that the horoscope is a reliable indicator of health matters. Maybe medical astrology was once a useful science; maybe there are still a few skilled practitioners of this all-but-lost art; but it is a very specialised and difficult matter, even if it works, which is debatable. As for the idea of every student including a health section in every Final Report.... We may get a few useful indications of general health from the overall psychological state of the person, but when it comes to specific ailments, astrologers must tread very carefully indeed. The usual significators seem to be Ascendant, Sun and Moon by sign, 1st house planets, 6th house planets, and certain aspects. I find the traditional correspondences of the Zodiac signs with the parts of the body as naively "logical" as the story of Noah's Ark: and by the time you have interpreted the list just quoted (and their opposites! For some unexplained reason, this system also works "by polarity" which means taking the opposite sign as well, regardless of the fact that in other contexts opposition means what it says: difference, conflict, challenge) you have identified virtually every part of the body and are liable to headaches, throat troubles, chest and nervous complaints, and so on through a weak heart down to bad feet. I have shown my chart to several experienced astrologers and asked them what ailment nearly cost me my life at age 18, and they never came near it. Have I succeeded in completely putting you off writing a Health section? Well, I may have done more good than harm.

8) Other matters. Astrology is totally unable to measure intelligence from a birthchart, in spite of textbooks which ascribe intelligence to such signs as Gemini or Aquarius. These signs may show an interest in mental activities, or a mental approach to life, but that is not the same thing. Astrology can cast *some* light on honesty, luck with money,

sex drive and creative ability, but cannot claim any real
degree of reliability in these matters.

THE NATURE OF ASTROLOGICAL INTERPRETATION

I am in no doubt that the whole corpus of meanings provided
by traditional astrology is a little unreal, in that it is slanted
towards many aspects of life which would never occur to us in
other situations. If we had to write a description of someone
we knew well, we would not be talking about legacies,
prisons, psychic ability or love of philosophy: more likely
about their sense of humour, likeability, intelligence or
perhaps political opinions; matters on which astrology is
perforce somewhat silent. If astrology is not well focused to
ordinary life, what is it good for, then? Well, it is not really
too far out of focus: there *is* a great deal of common ground
between an "everyday" description and a horoscopic interpretation: qualities such as steadfastness, sympathy, career
drive, social graces, adaptability, etc. etc. would appear in
both. But we would do well to reflect that, at bottom, all that
we derive from a birthchart is psychological in nature: we are
delving into a person's psychological makeup and drawing
further deductions from what we find. We must bear this in
mind at all times, and word our statements accordingly. This
does not contradict what I said above about avoiding
psychological terms: we must avoid using them, or at any rate
using them more than occasionally. What I want you to
realise is that the language of astrology (at its best) is really a
language of psychology, but one that is somewhat different
from that of established psychology: it has its own jargon
(what I call "astro-babble") and its own clichés which we
should take care not to pass on to the client. For example,
idealism is hardly a concept which we normally deal with in
our daily lives, and, whilst it might in some cases be a good
idea to bring a client face to face with his idealism or lack of it,
it is not so meaningful to most people as say the $64,000
problem of what they should devote their lives to. But
because there is a Neptune in every chart, and because we are

told that Neptune means idealism, we can all too easily find ourselves elaborating on "idealism" or "ideals" in every report that we write. If we made the imaginative leap out of astrological jargon into everyday ways of thinking, we could substitute "aim in life" for "idealism" and say something of more immediacy to our client.

STYLE OF WRITING

I have been trying to make clear, in the preceding pages, what sort of things we should avoid when writing our Final Report – the words that will actually be read by our client. But avoidance is negative, so let me try now to be positive, and say what you should be doing rather than what you should be avoiding. It seems to me that good style should have the following qualities:

1) It should be readily understood by the reader. Simple, straightforward language which gets to the point will automatically avoid puzzles, jargon and half-understood quotations. Make sure you put yourself in the reader's shoes: ask yourself after writing every sentence: "Is that pèrfectly clear? Could it possibly be misunderstood or read a different way?"

2) It should be in your own words. If you constantly copy phrases from books, the result will not only be an ugly hotch-potch of literary styles, but it will almost surely become obscure. Other people tend to write phrases which reflect a particular point of time and a particular relationship of writer/reader. Your writer/reader relationship is unique to you, this client and *now*. Quoting other people's phrases can be, at best, inappropriate to your situation, at worst totally incomprehensible. By all means refer to textbooks and use their information, but do translate it! If you do not understand what the author was saying, how do you expect your reader to understand? ("Dear client, please don't blame me; I got it from a very good textbook") And if you do understand, prove it by paraphrasing it into a wording that you are

prepared to take responsibility for. ("Yes, I wrote that. I meant so-and-so. Sorry I didn't make it clear.")

3) The style of writing should be appropriate to the age (which you know), socio-educational background and presumed level of intelligence (which you may have to guess from clues such as sound of voice, postal address and so on), and general experience of life (which you can infer from known details, eg. a sheltered housewife, a commercial traveller, a divorcee?). Thus you might try the exercise of interpreting the same chart as if to:

a) A teenage girl
b) A 30-year-old whose marriage is in difficulties
c) A 65-year-old who wants guidance on how to spend her declining years.

This sort of distinction is not something which can be easily taught and learnt (certainly I have little idea of how to guide you at this moment) but if you are alert to this point, and have some experience of life yourself, you can probably cope with it. If not, don't worry too much, it will come. By the way, unless you are very intimate with the client, do avoid the over-matey style which says such things as "Mary, my love,...." or "You see, my dear..." Not everyone will welcome uninvited cosiness. Be polite but friendly, formal without being starchy.

4) It should be tactful. I nearly wrote "at all times", but although tact is nearly always a good idea, there can be the fairly rare case where you feel that tact would be wasted and the client needs a firmly worded statement before he will listen. But make sure you know what you are doing in these cases! Know your person, know your occasion, be prepared for the comebacks...

But normally we should be concerned not to upset our client by being too blunt or even by being too truthful. So the question is bound to arise, quite often, of how frank we should be. Sometimes there are things which it is better for the astrologer to know about the client than to tell him: frankness might annoy or depress the client and defeat the object of astrology, which is to enrich life by greater self-knowledge. Where frankness might offend, you must weigh up both sides of the question: in avoiding offence you might fail your client by not telling him the very thing that could improve his life. Suppose he has come to you because he is perpetually quarrelling with his wife, and blames her for it; but you see from his chart that he is clearly a selfish and quarrelsome man. You do not say "You are selfish and quarrelsome. It is your fault." At least not in those words! But if you fail to get this message across, you will let him go away still thinking it is his wife's fault, and that is not fair on her. He *must* be told. Try something on the lines of "It is so easy for tempers to be lost when there are differences of opinion, isn't it? Happiness and peace depend on co-operation in trying to see the other person's point of view. I recommend you always to ask yourself, have I tried as hard to see the other person's point of view as hard as I expect them to try to see mine?" Now that I look at what I have just written I think perhaps it is not firm and clear enough; but then I am a man who tends to be more truthful than tactful, so I will leave it as it is. If you are the sort who is more tactful that truthful, you may have to look at some of your writings more carefully from the opposite angle: have you been so obsessed by tact that the real meaning passes unnoticed?

5) It should be of a reasonable length. Reasonable means not too long and not too short! One page of A4 is too short; twelve is almost certainly too long. If you find yourself unable to write a long report, ask yourself two questions: a) Did I generate enough meanings at the Notes stage? b) Can I expand my statements by giving examples of the qualities I am describing? ("You are generous by nature" can be expanded to "Another of your good qualities is generosity, whether of time or money. Friends know to turn to you when an extra pair of hands is needed: relations often get a warm

glow when your thoughtful little present arrives, and so on.")
If you think your reports are too long, ask yourself two
questions: a) Have I overdone the "padding by example"? b)
Have I included anything not derived from the chart? (Some
astrologers seem unable to resist preaching their purpose-in-
life-philosophy to the reader, or to give an unwanted essay on
reincarnation, or how astrology works, or to reiterate that
tiresome "You will grow wiser as you get older" message.)

6) It should be correct in spelling and grammar, and set out
with impeccable neatness. Too many astrologers let themselves and their profession down by semi-literate reports. For
example, do you write "You have a tendancy to be indepen-
dant."? (The correct spellings are "tendency" and "independent"). If so, why do you do it? Which is correct, "separate"
or "seperate"? And does it matter? Do you know when to
write "its" and when to write "it's"? Do you write "sentences"
like the following: "Adventurous, competitive, and strong of
purpose, following your own desires with perseverance."?
Are you unable to see what is what wrong with that?

If you are not totally confident of your ability to write correct
and clear English, then the remedy is in your hands. Don't be
content to spend the rest of your life blaming your poor
education for your deficiencies; take up classes at a local
evening institute or similar place, or get help from a more
literate friend. Take an interest in books, read more! At the
very least, have a dictionary by you when you write, and look
up any doubtful words.

A typewritten report has the best chance of looking neat and
readable. If this is impossible, make extra efforts to produce a
creditable result, as follows:
a) Use good quality paper, not a scruffy sheet torn from a pad
and showing a ragged edge or a pair of punched holes. Don't
use ordinary, small notepaper: quarto or A4 size is best. Go
to a good stationery shop and look around for something
suitable with ruled lines.
b) Leave adequate margins on all four sides of your text; also

break your text up into paragraphs of reasonable length and leave one or two lines between them. All this makes the result look more attractive, and is actually easier to read than a closely-packed script.

c) Write clearly, in your best handwriting. (Make sure you are not hampered by a poor, smudgy felt-tip pen or a hard scratchy ballpoint.) Tear it up and start again if you make a mess.

7) Statements should be made with an appropriate degree of caution. Hone recommends that a preface should always be affixed pointing out that nothing in the following document is to be taken as a firm claim to truth, only as a likelihood. One can follow this plan, and/or (preferably and) consider each and every sentence with a view to its "air of confidence". Are you saying that the client definitely *is* so-and-so? That such-and-such *will* happen? How do we avoid such traps as saying "You are..." when we are ever conscious that a person's character also depends on his environment and freewill? One way is to make use of phrases such as:

"You are probably..."
"I expect you..."
"Most likely you..."
"Perhaps.."
"Most of the time...."
"On the whole...."
"Possibly...."
"Sometimes..."
"Now and then..."
"You are more or less..."
"You tend to..."
"You can be .... at times"
"If you are not careful,..."
"Some people might think you ..."
"There is a danger that you might..."
"You might even..."
"Look out for a tendency to.."

And you can no doubt invent many others. The point I am trying to make is that we should freely avail ourselves of such phrases, not only to give variety to our style of writing, but to express something like the degree of uncertainty we may actually be feeling about a particular statement. If conflicting influences have ended in one "side" winning the synthesis battle, and we do not see fit to mention the losing tendencies, we may nevertheless be conscious of them, and so wish to hint at uncertainty in our phrasing.

On the other hand too many ifs, buts, and maybes are not only irritating to read, but undermine any confidence the client may have had in you; so where there is no reasonable doubt, make your statements confidently (not over-confidently! Use words like "definitely" with great care) and save the qualifying phrases for the places where you really feel caution is advisable. Another useful principle is to express doubt when describing personality faults, but to sound more positive about virtues: few clients will take offence at that!

8) As hinted at in the previous section, your text should show variety: variety of wording, variety of vocabulary, variety of sentence length, variety of mood. To elaborate:

Wording. Avoid too many sentences beginning "You ..." This may be difficult at first, but resolve to keep at it. Some alternatives: "Others find you..." "When it comes to ...." "In one-to-one situations you..." "Where work is concerned,..."

Vocabulary. Try to have a number of alternatives to common words that will keep cropping up. E.g. besides "very" say "rather", "somewhat", "quite", and so on. Besides "other people", use "others", "your friends", "your co-workers", "your fellowmen", "society", "strangers", "people you come across", or whatever may be appropriate.

Sentence length. Perhaps it has never occurred to you that continually reading sentences of approximately the same length is as boring as a ticking clock. Vary the length of your sentences. Also vary their internal construction: here's a bad example: "When in company you are charming and friendly. When at home you like peace and quiet. When out for the evening you seek excitement." If you can see nothing wrong with that, keep looking.

Mood. The prevailing mood of your report should be neutral most of the time. But if you can find a touch of humour here and there, it may help to make a point. (But don't go out of your way to crack jokes.) Choose your moment wisely: if there is something unpleasant to say, then a serious manner of writing is more appropriate. (Serious, not gloomy.)

WORKING WITH FEEDBACK

I suggest that you should now attempt some exercises in writing Final Reports. Do not attempt a complete one at first: take only one Category and try to make a good job of it. This can be done many times before trying to cope with all the categories at one attempt. The important thing is to try, after each exercise, to get some kind of feedback to see how well you are doing. First and foremost, read the whole thing over carefully when you have finished. Try to put yourself in the client's shoes, as if reading it for the first time. Do you spot any mistakes, contradictions, puzzles, or badly expressed passages? Is anything in the wrong section? When you can find nothing to improve, try to get someone else to read it. Ideally you would have an experienced astrology teacher looking over what you have written, and offering criticism, but failing that, ask a friend, particularly if it can be the person whose horoscope you are interpreting. Failing all the possibilities, put the work in a drawer for two weeks and then look at it yourself.

In all cases the aim of the feedback is to find out whether you are committing any of the faults outlined in this book, also whether you are making yourself clear, and (not least) whether the statements you are making about the person are accurate. Do not despair if you do badly: rewrite the offending section immediately, and again show it to your critic. The ultimate test is to write a complete Final Report for a friend, hand it to him, without his name on, and ask him who is being described. When he says "Why, that's me to the life!" you can feel you have reached a major milestone. From then on, it's a matter of experience making you better and quicker.

PRACTICE CHARTS
As a further help in this matter, I am now providing a couple of charts for you to practise on. I will give the chart data and also the complete Final Reports, so that you can compare your efforts with mine: the latter are given in Appendix 3. You can either do a category at a time, as just suggested, or do the whole job and then compare results. I have not shown all the intermediate stages because this would be more likely to confuse than to help. However, I have added a few notes to the Reports: these are aimed mainly at showing why the final wording took the form it did.

The identity of the natives has been concealed under false names and obviously ridiculous birthdata: I only give the latter so you have something to put in your main heading (but the year of birth is correct, to give you the age of the client). I don't give houses because I didn't use them, and I recommend that you don't, at least this time, so that the comparisons will be more meaningful. Of course if you like houses you are at liberty to use them in other contexts. In the first chart (Norman) I used the method of assessing strengths roughly, at three levels for planets and five for aspects: with Rowena I used an accurate numerical scoring system. Both methods are explained in Chapter 5. Incidentally, I used the following orbs for aspects:

Aspect	Degrees
Conj	8
Oppos	7
Trine	6
Square	5
Sextile	4
Semisq, Sesquisq	3
Semisext, Quincunx	2

One more thing: I made no attempt to generate a very large number of meanings from the chart factors: in both cases I got about 130 meanings – the reasonable minimum suggested earlier. So you shouldn't have too much difficulty getting a Final Report about the same length.

When you have finished the task and actually written the Final Report (make sure it is headed with what document it is, who it is for and who wrote it), then compare with mine. I do *not* expect you to get a result closely similar, but I do hope you will get one roughly similar, one which at any rate portrays the same person I am portraying. If you differ radically from me at any point, ask yourself why. Go back and check your intermediate workings: have you missed anything, or gone wrong in your arithmetic? Did you follow some unjustifiable "intuition" which has no basis in the chart? Of course you must remember that no two astrologers would produce precisely the same descriptions as each other. However, if you feel you have made a total hash of the job, why not get some more practice on your friends' charts, and then return to Norman and Rowena after a month or so? Try again; you should do better this time. (And you could also use Hone's "Applied Astrology" for further examples.) There's something important to remember, so important that I'll give it a paragraph to itself:

Astrology is always hard work. A complete natal interpretation is harder than most jobs, taking much time, care and

patience, not to mention reams of paper. Only the hard
workers succeed at it.

NATAL CHART FOR NORMAN

Born at Queryville on 31/2/41 at 3.45 am

Sun	7	Lib	23
Moon	16	Aqu	22
Merc	2	Sco	52
Venus	18	Sco	35
Mars	19	Ari	48
Jup	21	Gem	18
Sat	28	Tau	11
Ura	0	Gem	6
Nep	27	Vir	49
Plu	5	Leo	31
Asc	21	Can	38
MC	22	Pis	24

NATAL CHART FOR ROWENA

Born at Anyplace on 31/4/61 at 3.30 pm

Sun	19	Ari	59
Moon	11	Aqu	52
Merc	29	Pis	31
Venus	21	Ari	26
Mars	17	Can	23
Jup	4	Aqu	2
Sat	29	Cap	9
Ura	21	Leo	49
Nep	10	Sco	29
Plu	5	Vir	51
Asc	13	Cap	38
MC	20	Sco	36

N.B. Work out each of these charts to a Final Report
(complete or partial) *before* looking at Appendix 3.

APPENDICES

APPENDIX 1: KEYWORDS

The following lists, compiled from a selection of standard textbooks, should be found useful by the student. They are by no means exhaustive, the number of keywords having been deliberately kept to a minimum for ease of memorising, but anyone who learns them all will have a very useful core with which to work.

PLANETS
Sun
Power, Vitality, Self-expression, Real self, Willpower, Conscious aim, Yang principle, Creativity, Leadership, Pride, Ostentation, Domination.

Moon
Nurture, Habits, Childhood, The past, Mother, Wife, Home, Family, Yin principle, Emotional reactions, Subconscious, Moods, Instincts, Routine, Receptiveness, Memory.

Mercury
Mind, Communication, Reason, Logic, Learning ability, Analysis, Argument, Perceptiveness, Eloquence, Coordination, Adaptability, Ideas, Curiosity, Expressiveness, Interpretation, Restlessness, Routine travel, Dexterity, Nervous system.

Venus
Harmony, Relationships, Love, Beauty, Cooperation, Friendship, Romance, Agreement, Compromise, Empathy, Placidity, Young women, Arts, Pleasure, Vanity, Money, Luxury, Laziness.

Mars
Energy, Self-assertion, Action, Aggression, Survival urge, Force, Initiative, Enterprise, Impulse, Impatience, Quarrels, Masculinity, Young men, Sex, Courage, Cutting, Burning, Decisiveness.

Jupiter
Expansion, Wisdom, Optimism, Good luck, Tolerance, Generosity, Release, Religion, The law, Exploration, Higher learning, Flexibility, Enthusiasm, Conscience, Benevolence, Protectiveness, Lack of detail, Carelessness, Extravagance.

Saturn
Restriction, Discipline, Structure, Rigidity, Delay, Pessimism, Bad luck, Thrift, Stability, Old men, Authority figures, Concentration, Perseverance, Conventionality, Caution, Worry, Fear, Obstacles, Responsibility, Duty, Reliability, Self-restraint, Materialism.

Uranus
Deviation, Individuality, Independence, Originality, Science, Invention, Sudden events, Shock, Revolution, Progressiveness, Eccentricity, Freedom, Irresponsibility, Unpredictability.

Neptune
Intangibility, Idealism, Vagueness, Error, Deception, Intuition, Mystery, Creative imagination, Sacrifice, Confusion, Escapism, Refinement, Glamour, Illusion, Chaos, Dishonesty, Misunderstanding, Spiritual values, Visions, Occultism.

Pluto
Elimination, Regeneration, Decay, Rebirth, Transformation, Crisis, Destruction, Intensification, Obsession, Dictatorship, Orgasms, Large organisations, Underworld, Religious conversion, Psycho-analysis.

SIGNS

N.B. Although the following words are given as adjectives to save space, they are best thought of as adverbs. You can mentally add "-ly" to most of them, or of course you can put them in the correct form when making your notes.

Aries
Assertive, Selfish, Enthusiastic, Short-tempered, Energetic, Impatient, Urgent, Foolhardy, Impulsive, Aggressive.

Taurus
Possessive, Stubborn, Stable, Boring, Practical, Routine-bound, Reliable, Stodgy, Patient, Slow, Liking comforts, Greedy.

Gemini
Communicative, Superficial, Versatile, Inconstant, Quick learner, Lacks understanding, Inquisitive, Cunning, Witty, Two-faced.

Cancer
Protective, Moody, Nurturing, Smothering, Tender, Anxious, Tenacious, Touchy, Defensive, Clannish.

Leo
Impressive, Conceited, Self-confident, Arrogant, Seeking recognition, Overbearing, Dignified, Pompous, Leadership, Patronising.

Virgo
Perfectionist, Fastidious, Submissive, Over-modest, Efficient, Interfering, Detailed, Nit-picking, Precise, Pedantic, Analytical, Critical, Hygienic, Touch-me-not.

Libra
Cooperative, Vacillating, Diplomatic, Indecisive, Easygoing, Frivolous, Art-loving, Lacking confidence, Peaceable, Too soft, Loving, Dependent.

Scorpio
Intense, Fanatical, Dramatic, Destructive, Mysterious, Suspicious, Subtle, Covert, Purposeful, Vindictive.

Sagittarius
Adventurous, Careless, Idealistic, Extravagant, Freedom-loving, Exaggerative, Wise, Moralistic, Jovial, Tactless.

Capricorn
Disciplined, Stern, Conventional, Narrow-minded, Serious, Pessimistic, Careful, Calculating, Prudent, Mean, Ambitious, Callous.

Aquarius
Objective, Unemotional, Gregarious, Aloof at heart, Progressive, Casual, Scientific, Perverse, Reformative, Rebellious.

Pisces
Imaginative, Confused, Impressionable, Passive, Compassionate, Impractical, Self-effacing, Elusive.

HOUSES
1st
The person, Outward appearance, Self-image, Physical appearance, Temperament, Image others see, Personal interests.

2nd
Possessions, Feelings, Money, Property, Earning & spending, Personal security, Attitude to material values.

3rd
Mental interests, Short journeys, Immediate environment, Nearest relatives, Neighbours, Manner of speech, Ability to learn, Routine communications.

4th
Home, Early environment, Childhood, Upbringing, Private life, Mother, The end of things, The womb, The tomb.

5th
Creativity, Self-expression, One's children, Amusements, Recreations, Love affairs, Speculation, Gambling, Being a parent, Artistic creations.

6th
Work, Service, Health, Efficiency, Routine, Day-to-day employment, Pets.

7th
Partnerships, Marriage, Cooperation, Enemies, Confrontations, Oppositions, One-to-one relationships.

8th
Regeneration, Shared possessions, Death/birth experiences, Occult matters, Other people's money, Legacies, The lifeforce.

9th
Long journeys, Higher understanding, Philosophy, Religion, Law, Foreign affairs, Widening experiences.

10th
Public life, Career, Social status, Reputation, Attainment, Goals, Authority figures, Father.

11th
Friendships, Group activities, Hopes, Wishes, Social ideals.

12th
Hidden affairs, Selfless service, Secrets, The unconscious, Escapism, Confinement, Karma, Sacrifice, Retirement.

APPENDIX 2: FINAL REPORT:
HEADINGS & SUBHEADINGS

Note: These are intended as suggestions and guidelines, not as a rigid system. See page 36 for further details.

1) General character
a) Disposition. (Restlessness, enthusiasm, competitiveness, calmness, impressionability, sentimentality, selfishness, independence.)
b) Emotions. (Intensity, stability, control, temper, ability to communicate feelings.)
c) Inner qualities. (Integrity, sense of justice, mature outlook, nobility, courage.)
d) Guiding principles. (Self-interest, perfectionism, superficiality, willpower, conservatism, response to duty, variety, sense of responsibility, initiative, perseverance, constancy.)
e) Manner of action. (Energy, compulsive manner, patience, caution, speed of action, openness, self-discipline, methodicalness, care, neatness, efficiency, orthodoxy, practicality, reliability, exaggerativeness, unpredictability, versatility.)
f) Outer personality. (Optimism, outgoingness, pleasantness, refinement, mysteriousness, dignity, self-importance, dramatic manner, liveliness, manner of dress.)

2) Mentality
a) Abilities. (Activeness, originality, ingenuity, memory, speed of thought, decisiveness, clarity, complexity, wisdom, commonsense, mental discipline, attention to facts, logicality, sense of structure, sense of details, practicality of ideas, concentration, powers of analysis and problem-solving, foresight, planning.)

b) Less tangible qualities. (Imagination, dreaminess, intuition, psychic ability, inspiration, idealism.)

c) Beliefs. (Based on reason, reached carefully, reached quickly, sound and reliable, broadmindedness, tolerance, firmly-held opinions, moral values, strict attention to rules.)

d) Mental attitudes. (Surface self-confidence, inner self-confidence, relaxed mind, introspection, objectivity, scheming, ulterior motives, philosophical attitude, self-awareness, conceit.

e) Learning. (Ability to study, speed, curiosity, educational handicaps.)

f) Communication (N.B. This may be treated as a separate section if your prefer.) (Fluency, talkativeness, good expression, frankness, truthfulness, misleading, misunderstood, exaggerative, critical, argumentative, sarcastic, witty, fond of jokes, trivial talk.)

3) Recreations and career

a) General recreations. (Sport, travel, entertainment, mental games, arts, sciences.)

b) Particular recreations. (One or two from about 20 specific hobbies to be suggested.)

c) General careers. (Maths, science, languages, management, craft, engineering, sales, public relations, travelling, caring, children.)

d) Particular careers (Three or four from about 25 particular careers.)

e) Style of work. (Whether unconventional, with other people, in partnership, under authority, in large firm, in public eye, relations with co-workers, able to cope with boring routine.)

f) Efficiency. (Businesslike, efficient, hardworking, reliable.)

g) Progress. (Career drive, ambition for authority, need for fame, general success, many job changes, reward for effort.)

4) Social Relationships

a) Friends chosen. (Attracted to what type of people, group activities, group leader.)

b) Approach to personal relationships. (Social conformity, friendliness, gregariousness, ability to form new friendships, number of friends, length of friendships, charm, kindness, generosity, quarrelsomeness, argumentativeness, modesty, suspiciousness, condescension, humanity, warmth, can compromise, cooperative, discreet, tactful.)

c) Social behaviour. (Self-effacement, liking for admiration, expecting favours, using flattery, receptiveness to advice, understanding, sympathy, anxiety to please, wetblanket, readiness to help, ability to keep promises, imposing own moral values, respected.)

d) Social problems. (Involvement in deception, paranoic tendencies, quickness to take offence, forgiveness, attitude to injustice, expression of anger, ease of being "understood", tendency to play martyr, ease of manipulation.)

5) Love and marriage

a) Falling in love. (Ability to get on with opposite sex, sex appeal, fidelity, number of affairs, falling in love quickly, secret affairs, critical of loved one, dominating, idealistic in love, over-smothering, feeling unloved, able to let go finished affair.)

b) Showing love. (Ardour, stability of affections, expression, need of affection, jealousy, possessiveness.)

c) Sex. (Strong sex drive, inhibitions, responsiveness, physical side, sex as manipulation.)

d) Marriage. (Probability, lateness in life, type of partner, sharing in responsibilities, likelihood of happiness, likeliness of divorce.)

6) Domestic and other matters

a) Money. (Desire for material wealth, joint finances, thrift, wisdom in spending, steadiness of financial state, speculation.)

b) Home. (Energy spent on it, how much a tie, type of home, frequency of moving house, ability to cope with domestic routine, attitude to family, entertaining friends, relationship with parents.)

c) Children. (Fondness for, probable type, problems, protective to, discipline.)

d) Health. (General level, careful with health, liability to fatigue, care with sharp tools, avoidance of alcohol.)

7) Life Attitude

a) Main object in life. (Prestige, excitement, glamour, romance, harmony, power, security, benefitting humanity.)

b) Best point. (Good intentions, strong principles, fights for right, adaptable, desires self-improvement, spiritual development.)

c) Chief drawback. (Over-ambition, over-importance, out-of-date attitudes, indiscreet behaviour, too many activities, superficiality, poor timing.)

d) Dominant behaviour pattern. (Using force, taking risks, promoting a cause, worshipping a guru, fanaticism, changing life-style readily, trying to alter others, sacrificing self.)

e) Ultimate aim. (Happiness, doing right thing, being loved, achieving.)

APPENDIX 3: FINAL REPORTS FOR NORMAN & ROWENA

See page 71

Horoscope for NORMAN By Terry Dwyer

Born in Queryville on 31 February 1941 at 3.45 am [1]

Sun in Libra
Moon in Aquarius
Ascendant Cancer   [2]

Character

You would seem to be of a reasonably stable disposition, though you have plenty of energy and enthusiasm at your disposal. Your feelings are not normally very powerful, thus helping you to keep on an even keel emotionally; however you do sometimes get a sudden rush of feeling if the situation provokes it, then your emotions run quite high for a time—quite disconcerting for you, probably.

In outlook you tend to the conservative view of life, preferring to follow tradition where possible, and proving rather unresponsive to new ideas: thus you are unlikely to be much of an innovator yourself. [3]

When first going into action your energy seems boundless;

your keenness to succeed in whatever you are doing shows as an optimistic, eager attack on the task, and indeed you can accomplish many endeavours quite successfully. However, it must be said that you are somewhat dependent upon other people for support (whether actual or moral), and would be very much more cautious about undertaking tasks if you felt on your own. Actually you might well initiate a project if it would bring you a personal advantage, but if the task were for other people to profit by, your willpower would be strong only whilst things were going well and other people were agreeing with what you were doing. It would be difficult for you to take the role of the pioneer who stands alone in his convictions.

You have a problem: although you are impulsive and impatient to begin things, you tend to take a casual, easy-going approach in tackling jobs, using a somewhat individual approach, in spite of your respect for tradition. However, you are willing to compromise in method, should the need for this become apparent. All in all, this adds up to the fact that you are rather apt to rush into action without sufficient planning.

The impression you give to others is a little ambivalent: chiefly you radiate a cheerful, infectious optimism; but an underlying fearfulness is also apparent (it's a *nervous* optimism), and the general impression you leave is that you underestimate the difficulties that face you, and overestimate your own capability to tackle them. What people do not easily realise is your ability to pick yourself up from a fall, time after time: more of this later. [4]

Mentality
There is a strong intellectual slant to your horoscope, so the world of the mind is important to you. You have an intense curiosity and desire to learn. "Knowledge is power" would be one of your beliefs, and you constantly seek wisdom and understanding of life, in a broad way. There is a danger here:

in pursuing your broad ideal vision of wisdom you certainly acquire a good general knowledge, but this vaguely progressive attitude makes it difficult for you to specialise successfully in any one subject. You are certainly capable of concentrated study of one thing at a time, but at the end of the day it is difficult for you to hold fast to one guiding belief and follow it. However, this breadth of vision certainly makes you tolerant of other people and their views.

You have good imagination, which you have under control. Your mind is mainly objective, so that you can examine other people's ideas on their merits: however, your own ideas are sometimes a bit odd; you hold to them fanatically and spend time planning how you may make them come true. Lacking a certain amount of mental confidence, you can be tempted to believe that these ideas can only be implemented by the help of some carefully planned (and possibly secret) scheme. What you should do, of course, is share your ideas with someone who can help you see them as objectively as you see other people's.

Indecisiveness is a problem generally. You are anxious to make decisions, especially where your personal affairs are involved, but are much inclined to vacillate and hesitate. This is not because you see both sides of a question (in fact you lean towards one-sided reasoning) but because you are not confident of the outcome of your decision. If only you could be *sure* that it was the right one and that there would be no comebacks! However, once a decision is taken it is a great relief for you and you are fired with enthusiasm to get on and implement it.

In speech and writing you are much concerned to communicate the wisdom and knowledge you have acquired. You tend to do this in a dramatic, excited manner.

Recreations & career
You would appear to incline towards intellectual pastimes like reading and conversation or debate, also towards artistic

84

subjects such as painting, drama or music. In fact you seem to have a special leaning towards music, and possibly some creative ability here.

Because of your intellectual slant and desire to communicate your knowledge, you are suited to the career of teacher (especially of music or art) or perhaps as art critic, author, or musicologist, etc. The nutshell of your ideal job can be expressed as "The opportunity to pass on my acquired knowledge of artistic, musical and philosophical matters".

Your general approach to work can be deduced from my remarks in the first (Character) section above: after an eager start your generally easy-going approach and casual, occasionally lazy routines would undermine your efficiency if you were not very careful. Your enthusiasm is obvious but your superiors would be looking for sustained efforts, not to mention results. So do try to see your tasks through to a suitable conclusion.

You would have a unique way of working, breaking rules to suit yourself, yet wanting to impose your own methods somewhat rigidly on others. Although you have some respect for authority, you are quite likely to have misunderstandings with those above you, and sometimes to be involved in friction with your boss. You could work very well with a partner.

In short, the easiest mistake for you to make (assuming a career in, say, teaching) would be to assume that because you have good knowledge which you continue to improve throughout your life, you are necessarily passing this on properly. Time spent on planning your work would repay you over and over again.

Social relationships
You are fond of company, though unlikely to become close to many people. Most likely you would gravitate to

strongwilled, intense people or to active, hardworking, reliable types. [5]

You are certainly co-operative and diplomatic, very willing to compromise and preaching tolerance. These are excellent virtues but they can be overdone, and you need to guard against overdoing them to the extent that you may seem to have no mind of your own, going with the majority or whatever may seem expedient at the time.

You give off a generous, helpful, caring image. Tact comes easily, and seldom if ever would you be rude or give offence. You can be a bit touchy sometimes, but your natural inclination towards tact and co-operation means that you would try to conceal that someone has just offended you.

Love and marriage
The limitation on the number of your close friends certainly applies to your love-life too. The way to your heart travels through a barrier of reserve, even suspicion. Once there, a loved one would be guarded possessively and cherished intensely. As a matter of fact you have a strongly sexual nature.

You would tend to find a wife who would be a little cool in affection, and perhaps preoccupied with trivialities. She would meet you intellectually but might not share your grand philosophical views.

There might be problems in your love life: indeed there could be problems with women in general, though I cannot specify their precise nature.

Domestic matters
You are at your best at home, where you would be active and happy. The activity could well take the form of DIY improvements; in any case you would try to have a beautiful house, one you could be proud of. You are likely to spend more than you can afford on domestic improvements.

You are co-operative with your family, and you like having visitors. Home is also a place where you would enjoy study and learning.

Life Attitude

The keynote of your life is an impatience to succeed, coupled with a vagueness where responsibility is concerned. Your anxiety to do well in life can result in your setting yourself targets for which you are not really suited. In other words, you haven't weighed up the cost properly. You may feel held back by circumstances and thus want to seek freedom on a higher plane (or in a better job) but the freedom is illusory: better jobs mean more responsibility and more onus on you to "carry the can". Are you really suited to stand alone? If you are content to realise your limitations in this respect, you could aim instead at more *mental* freedom and expansion. Perhaps after all you would be happiest as a research scholar working loosely within a small team. Or if this is not possible, personal study as a hobby would give you enough contentment to tolerate whatever else may be unsatisfactory.

One last thing: in a real crisis you are a survivor, having the ability to start out in a completely new direction and stand on your own feet for a while. [6] Of course, when the dust settles you will be once again anxious for moral support from those around you. One can never quite escape one's basic make-up!

Keep the enthusiasm coming; it's a terrific asset. You'll always get a kick out of life so long as there are still jobs to be done. [7]

Terry Dwyer [8]
7 Jan 1985

NOTES

1) Did you remember to identify your document properly?

2) Optional: most people would like this.

3) A slightly padded expression of one basic idea, to prevent the paragraph from looking too thin.

4) Although this anticipates a point in Life Attitude, it is included here to cheer him up a bit.

5) Using Venus sign and Descendant sign.

6) Avoiding the "astro-babble" word "regeneration".

7) An extra little paragraph given so as to end on a positive note.

8) Signed, not typed.

Horoscope for ROWENA by Terry Dwyer

Born in Someplace on 31st April 1961 at 3.30 pm

Sun in Aries
Moon in Aquarius
Ascendant Capricorn

Character

It can be said from the outset that your driving force is a desire to accomplish – to feel, eventually, that you have achieved something in life. More, you must feel that you alone have done this, and your strongly independent nature makes you refrain from asking help from others—or perhaps, to put it more accurately, you don't entirely realise the value of co-operation. Your natural instinct is to see all problems from your own standpoinť and to attempt to solve them without sufficient reference to the world around you: the virtue of this is self-reliance but the danger is a self-centred attitude. [1]

You seem to have a variable disposition, with a temperament mostly calm and stolid, but sometimes fired with enthusiasm or even highly-strung. It is not easy for you, or for those around you, to cope with this instability of mood, especially when you are nervous or perversely obstinate, as indeed you sometimes are. Your temper can be a little short, and often influenced by your unconscious mind, so that it is possible to find you in a "bolshy" mood when you are hard to please for no apparent reason.

But you mean well! You are honest, fair and straight-dealing with people. You would rather call a spade a spade than be devious, and would never be sly or deceptive. [2] It's only when your emotions get the better of you that you let yourself down. In general you are strongwilled and conscientious, and prefer to go deeply into most matters. You have a great sense of responsibility and the ability to keep your sights on your goal without wavering; to persevere to the finish.

You have plenty of energy—and a problem in using it. The energy is often available in urgent form, and impulsive behaviour can result. Yet a strong part of your make-up needs to act in a disciplined, cautious way, so there is a tussle. Maybe sometimes one side wins, sometimes the other, but on the whole I judge that caution predominates and that you operate mainly in a careful manner, hating to leave anything to chance. Of course there is a price to pay for suppressing the urgent impatience, and so you will often appear rather anxious when in action.

A similar ambivalence shows in another matter: generally you have a conventional approach to life and would tend to follow well-trodden paths—yet there is also a strongly individual streak which means you would like to implement tradition in your own particular way.

You are outgoing by nature and try to project a cheerful image, though this has a bit of a struggle getting through the aura of serious dignity which you cannot help giving off, try as you may. Oh well, there's nothing wrong with semi-cheerful dignity!

Mentality
Just as you attempt to control your impulses with cautious action, so you probably try to control your mental processes.

But you are not naturally a quick or easy thinker; logic comes hard to you and thinking is normally a little on the slow side. Vague thinking is easiest, for you have a fertile imagination (even a touch of inventiveness) and daydreaming is frequent. Mental fantasies are indulged in, and you would rather follow a hunch than do what logic demands (you are not always sure what logic demands). Thought processes are calm but easily confused. You are fairly decisive, but decisions are affected by feelings, which are not always reliable. All the same you try hard to be a realist, without letting go of your ideals entirely. You enjoy dreaming about your ideal life, but you know in your heart you have to get down to work if you want to have it.

This constant struggle with elusive thoughts means that you are apt to overlook details, yet you hold very firmly to your opinions, once formed. What else can you do? It seems the easiest way to conquer the doubts you may have, for without much doubt you are a born worrier. Careful, though! You can appear somewhat intolerant and dogmatic, and give the impression of a narrow-minded person, simply because you tend to the conventional, and because you are hard to shift, once you hold a view.

Where learning is concerned, there is little real curiosity. Your mind is passive and impressionable, so you are capable of picking up knowledge, but only if you are interested: it would be difficult to make a sustained effort to learn an uncongenial subject, and learning is in any case slow and a little error-prone.

In speech, your words would be carefully considered and delivered in a sober, undramatic fashion. In any case you don't normally have a lot to say, for you are a doer rather than a talker. Conversations tend to be on unimportant subjects rather than on the deep issues of life.

Recreations & career
There are no really clear indications as to the kind of spare-time activities which would best suit you. There may some

liking for sport: it there isn't, it is worth remembering what a good outlet physical games can be whenever you are feeling tense or dissatisfied.

Probably you would spend time on personal entertainments such as films, television, meals out and dances, etc. You like a bit of fun, provided you also feel you are getting your money's worth.

There is also some slight indication of a liking for unusual art. You would tend to prefer slightly offbeat pictures and decorations: you might even have a little artistic ability.

You would not be a great one for travelling, I expect: if you did get around it would be mostly for short journeys. You should prefer ground or sea travel to flying, even though it is slower. [3]

Nor is any specific career indicated. However, it is clear that you would be happy working in a safe, probably large establishment where you could work your way up by promotion over the years. Possibly the Civil Service, or a bank or large industrial firm would provide suitable opportunities. Other alternatives are a solicitor's clerk or a librarian. You respond well to routine work, and can follow orders happily. You would bring a disciplined approch to your job, and perform it efficiently and reliably.

Securing the co-operation of your fellow-workers might be a problem: see if you can find a job which allows you to work on your own: you would in any case enjoy the responsibility.

All in all, you are likely to have a successful career, with few job changes.

Social relationships
Social activity makes you happy, and you like to be surrounded by people: not too many at a time though, because you do like to have your share of attention in company—in fact, to be honest, you probably like having

more than your share. You are anxious to be liked, and put a lot of energy into your social life. There is some leadership ability, even if you are not aware of it.

A basically democratic approach underlies your social life; for you are tolerant of many different life-styles, and believe that no-one should have too many privileges not shared by others. You adopt a friendly and sympathetic attitude to those you meet, and your normal manner is courteous. However, you can be tactless sometimes without realising it.

Others find you quite attractive, for you have an indefinable personal magnetism. You don't really need all those cosmetics or fashionable clothes you buy! (though of course, they give you pleasure, don't they?) You are quite active in making friendships, often forming attachments quite impulsively.

Once relationships are formed, your friends find that you can appear a little forbidding sometimes, or even callous. (For all your apparent sympathy, you are unlikely to put yourself out much for others.) They have to realise that you are only being fair and honest according to your lights, and if they choose to feel hurt, well.... On different occasions you might suddenly make a generous gesture. You probably make it on principle, again because it seems fair; fortunately your friends will take it as spontaneous warmth. They really do want to love you, in spite of your inner doubts about your self-worth.

This self-doubting is also responsible for the occasions when you get a bit touchy, having taken offence at some remark or act which was never intended to hurt you. Please remember that you can be over-sensitive, and make allowances for this.

One more of your little weaknesses is argumentativeness. Unfortunately you are prone to seeing only one side of most controversies, and you do like to get your own way when paths cross; so there can be sudden flare-ups (quite surprising to those who only know your restrained manner), and you can waste time in a verbal battle which nobody wins. In particular you are likely to get involved in quarrels with men, so there's a point to watch out for: next time a man upsets you, ask yourself who really started it.

What all this really adds to, Rowena, is, is that you don't need to work so hard at being liked. Yes, surprising as it may seem, being tetchy with others is a disguised form of saying "You don't really love me, do you?" Now, the finest and surest way to feel loved is to do some loving yourself. Those last two words are a bit ambiguous: don't love yourself too much! What I am saying is that if your make sure to *show* other people that you care about them and that their happiness is as important as yours, it all comes home to roost, and you find that you will receive love, and what is more, feel really good about it. The nigger in the woodpile here is your basic need for independence: this, too, contributes to difficulties in human relationships because it makes it harder to give and receive love; for after all, every relationship implies dependence of one kind or another. For you it may even be as hard to receive as to give.... [4]

Love and marriage
It should be clear from the above that your are likely to have many acquaintances and friends but there will be few people with whom you can feel really close. And I have to say that your tendency to clash with men will create problems in your love life, but they are far from insuperable. You have a lot going for you, including terrific sex appeal. [5]

You are apt to fall in love quite swiftly, and the other side of this penny is that you may tire of your lover just as quickly. So expect quite a few affairs before you settle down. Romance must be exciting for you, so it is important that your final partner has the right qualities. You will be happiest with a protective, caring, co-operative man; but he must also possess some sparkle, some out-of-the-rut quality which will make him perennially interesting to you.

You have a strong, uninhibited sex drive, an intensely passionate nature, and an affectionate disposition (when you are not hiding it with the sterner side of your nature.) All this means that your partner must be prepared for plenty of loving! Your need to work off steam in your love life may even lead to your making him feel smothered if your are not careful, so ease up now and then. You easily feel unloved, remember, and what you may take for a cold lack of response on his part may be no more than a need for breathing-space.

In any case you will benefit from a marriage which leaves a certain amount of freedom to each partner—not for infidelity but for feeling that each need not account for every movement they make. You should not find this difficult, for I do not believe you are possessive in love, in spite of your inner passion. Do not be surprised if from time to time you will need to look at your marriage and reappraise its nature, perhaps to change things in some way. This does not imply divorce; it simply means that your are not prepared for a humdrum wedlock, preferring one which can be updated to your mutual needs. Your marriage will always be happy if you keep the sparkle alive.

Domestic matters
You have two inclinations where money is concerned: half of you knows how important it is to save, or spend wisely; the other half loves spending impulsively, especially on luxuries. If only you were a millionaire the problem would be solved! However, money will not come easily, so I expect you will take a balanced view as most people do, being mostly prudent but with the odd fling. Why not?

I see you as quite active in the home, making it a place you like to come back to after a hard day's work. Perhaps you are a little casual about housework, though, and may forget the odd chore or be a little untidy... Yet you would really love an unusual, individually furnished home. You will probably not move house often.

94

Remember that short temper I mentioned above, too. There is some possibility that home is the most likely place for it to surface, particularly after a difficult day at the office. Somehow home is a place where you feel you can let rip your frustrations. I expect you had a few quarrels with your parents in the past, particularly your father. All too easily your family can feel that you are a little aloof, so be sure to keep in touch with them.

Your health should be quite good. Just watch out you don't overtire yourself: it is particularly important to get plenty of rest and relaxation when you are at home. Go easy on alcohol; it is not particularly good for you.

Life attitude
Your anxiety to succeed in life is matched by a desire for glamorous or romantic pursuits. These two do not easily go together, so expect a certain amount of inner, apparently irrational discontent. And be prepared for the growth of prosperity to be slow; you must not expect quick results. Your peak time will be comparatively late in life, when the rough edges of youth have been softened, and experience and wisdom show their fruits. Much toil may have to take place, and unforeseen snags dealt with, before you feel you have reached the haven of security you crave. Then you will be free to enjoy the company of the many friends you will have made along the route. [6]

Terry Dwyer
10 January 1985

NOTES

1) The opening sentence belongs more properly to the Life Attitude section, but the word at the top of my sorted notes was "Selfish". One could hardly start with a blunt statement to this effect, so this paragraph was written to lead up to selfishness as a *danger*.

2) High time to supply some virtues!

3) Actually, *because* it is slower.

4) Much of this paragraph would be omitted if Rowena were middle-aged.

5) "Terrific" is an exaggeration, but she needs an ego-boost after the faults which have been referred to.

6) Again, these are age-dependent comments.

WHY NOT LET YOUR
COMPUTER HELP?

If you have a home computer, you could be using two splendid programs written by Terry Dwyer to make chart interpretation easier. The first one has been referred to in the text of this book:

REMARK SORTER
A remarkable aid to writing any kind of interpretation, and as useful to the busy professional as to the beginner. You need a printer attached to your computer. What the program does is as follows:

1) Lets you type in any number of "remarks", i.e. comments, abbreviated notes or whatever. You precede each remark by a code letter such as C for Character, L for Love and so on. This can be done as you work direct from the birthchart.

2) When you signal the end of the comments, the computer immediately sorts them into their respective categories and prints them out under those headings. Some people might stop here, but there is more if you wish:

3) Examine each category and decide in what order you want the notes, within the category. Mark each comment with a number, accordingly. Tell all this to the computer as it prompts you, and when you have finished:

4) All remarks are once again printed out, this time in the final order you wanted. You can now proceed with writing up the notes into a Final Report, confident that you have brought the proper notes together.

5) There is more! By using a simple code, you can get the

computer to automatically add the source of the remark (eg Mars square Uranus) and/or a strength score: these extras will faithfully be reproduced in the final printout so that you can assess which of conflicting factors are the strongest. Once you use the Remark Sorter program you will wonder how you ever managed without it.

SYNTHESIS

A truly revolutionary concept in astrocomputing. A program which actually teaches you the art of analysis and synthesis by taking you through every step, inviting you to make decisions and then telling you if you were right. It can even interpret a chart all by itself, though it is best used as a means of practising your own skills.

Ten practice charts, arranged in order of difficulty, reside permanently in the memory, or you can enter any chart of your own choice. You don't have to tackle the whole chart at first, in fact you can choose just how much you want to work on: anything from one planet or one aspect, upwards.

You are invited to judge the strength of each planet by angularity, and the strength of each aspect; then you are asked to select which of 84 traits apply to the factor you are working on. When all chosen chart factors have been analysed, you start synthesis. Each trait is displayed, together with all the chart factors that bear on it, and you decide the final outcome (exactly as described in the book "How to write an Astrological Synthesis"). The computer scores you, and you can try again and again until you improve.

Final output is in the form of brief notes which can be amplified. A printer is not essential for this program, but can be used to make a permanent record if required. A 20-page instruction booklet accompanies the program.

ASTROCALC
British Astrological Software
The above programs are marketed by Astrocalc, the leading astrosoftware firm in Europe, and are available for most home computers. For full details of these and other programs for astrologers, send a large sae to:

Astrocalc
67 Peascroft Road
Hemel Hempstead
Herts HP3 8ER